Succeed in College!

Succeed in College!

WALTER PAUK

Director, Reading Research Center
Cornell University

JOHN P. FIORE

University of Illinois

Houghton Mifflin Company   Boston   New York

Senior Sponsoring Editor: Kerry Baruth
Associate Editor: Marianne Stepanian
Senior Project Editor: Janet Young
Editorial Assistant: Nasya Laymon
Senior Manufacturing Coordinator: Priscilla Bailey
Marketing Manager: Pamela Laskey

Cover designed by Rebecca Fagan

Printed in the U.S.A.

ISBN: 0-618-21989-7

10-QUF-07 06 05 04 03

Contents

To the Student

This book was designed to help you achieve success, not only in your introductory psychology course, but throughout your college career. Four of the five chapters were derived from the bestselling college study skills text, *How to Study in College,* Fourth Edition, by Professor Walter Pauk of Cornell University. The chapters present effective methods for mastering areas of interest to every student—managing time, taking good notes, learning from textbooks, and performing well on tests. More than one million students have used Walter Pauk's text in its first three editions. Now you can benefit from the Pauk approach to study skills.

The fifth chapter in this book, "Psychology and Careers," provides valuable information on majoring in psychology and making use of a psychology degree. Written by Dr. John P. Fiore of the University of Illinois, the chapter examines a wide range of career opportunities and identifies the college courses that can put you on various career paths.

Succeed in College! has been prepared exclusively to accompany *Psychology,* by Bernstein, Clarke-Stewart, Penner, Roy, and Wickens, and is available only with this textbook.

Here's to your success in college psychology—and beyond!

Succeed in College!

CHAPTER 1

Controlling Your Time

YESTERDAY is a canceled check.
TOMORROW is a promissory note.
TODAY is ready cash. Use it!

Anonymous

Time flies, but that's no reason for you to go through each day simply "winging it." Through conscientious use of time and common-sense planning, you can make the most of your day. This chapter ticks off the important elements of time management, including

- Mastering time
- Scheduling time to gain time
- Principles of scheduling
- Types of schedules
- Scheduling for students with jobs
- Tips for saving time
and finally
- Getting things done

Your success or failure in college depends directly on your use of time. If you use it wisely, you'll prosper. If you use it poorly, you'll fail in the job you came to do. The management of time is the number-one skill to master in college.

Anyone who has paid $30 an hour (50 cents a minute) for a plumber knows that time means money. Actually, time is worth far more than money. Time is life itself, and no price can be put on that. The preciousness of time has never been evoked more convincingly and more succinctly than in the final words of Elizabeth I (1533–1603), queen of England:

All my possessions for a moment of time.

MASTERING TIME

If you want to take control of your life, you must take control of your time. Golda Meir, a schoolteacher in Milwaukee, went on to become prime minister of Israel. Her success was due in part to how she dealt with time. She said, "I must govern the clock, not be governed by it." In order to be the master of time instead of its slave, you must have a *goal*, you must have a *plan*, and you must *take action*.

Formulating a Goal

Nothing will fortify your inner self more than setting personal goals. To succeed in almost anything, you must have a goal. You have to know what you want to be before you can become it, and if you don't know where you're going, you won't get there. Goal setting is not kid stuff. It's student power! It's adult power!

Successful people in all walks of life realize the importance of setting goals. Businesspeople put their goals in writing. They have to show their weekly, monthly, and yearly goals to their immediate supervisors. Even the president of a corporation has to write goals and submit them to the board of directors. Setting goals is almost instinctive behavior. Pioneers heading west painted "California or Bust" on their covered wagons. This slogan was not a magic carpet whisking them across the continent, but it was a constant reminder of their goal.

You *must* express your goal in writing, on a sheet of paper. Your goal should be more specific and less general than simply getting a college education. You need to formulate a clear notion of not only *what* you want in college and life but also *why* you want it. Writing is important. The act of writing will help you clarify your thoughts.

No matter what you want to become—a computer programmer, sales manager, a civil engineer, a teacher, a dentist, a journalist—put your goal in writing and work to achieve it. As a college student you will have to weather some very rough days, and at times things may seem to be falling apart. That's when you'll need a lifeline to hold onto. Focusing on your goal can give you the perspective and strength you need to keep going.

Making a Plan

A plan is the route or approach you want to take in order to reach your goal. A record sheet such as the one shown in Figure 1.1 will help you devise your plan.

On a separate sheet of paper jot down all that comes to mind regarding your goal. Summarize these jottings in a brief statement, and transfer that statement to block 1 in Figure 1.1.

Keeping your goal in mind, on a separate sheet jot down the steps that you must take to reach your goal. Select from your jottings the steps that lead directly to your goal, and list them in block 2 in Figure 1.1.

On another separate sheet list positive factors that will help you accomplish your goal. It helps a lot to know what's working for you. Once you've identified these factors, add them to block 3.

You need to face reality, so think about the problems and obstacles that you have to overcome to reach your goal. List them in block 4.

With your record sheet in hand, take the next step of talking to your academic adviser as well as to a counselor in the career center. Don't underestimate the value of thinking about, writing about, and discussing your goal and plan. Get as much discussion and feedback as you can; then modify your plan if necessary. You will end up with a plan for your future that is realistic and attainable.

Taking Action

Among the saddest words in life are "It might have been." If you take no action, your goals and plans will amount to nothing. Taking action, however, is more easily said than done. In order to take action, you will need a large dose of self-discipline. Adapting to military discipline might even be easier than imposing discipline on yourself, yet self-discipline is what you must have if you are to take the action required to implement your plans. For instance, let's say your particular goal is to excel in your biology course. You think you

1

My Goal
_____
_____
_____
_____
_____
_____
_____

2

Positive Factors

1. _____
2. _____
3. _____
4. _____
5. _____
6. _____
7. _____

3

Steps Leading to My Goal

1. _____
2. _____
3. _____
4. _____
5. _____
6. _____
7. _____

4

Obstacles

1. _____
2. _____
3. _____
4. _____
5. _____
6. _____
7. _____

FIGURE 1.1 **Record Sheet for Planning**

may have trouble with some of the terms and concepts, so you've decided to seek the assistance of a department tutor. The department identifies the tutor for you, and now it's up to you to contact him or her. If you procrastinate here, all the time and thinking that went into your plan will have been wasted. Taking action simply means taking those steps necessary to complete your plan. When you identify a task, you must go ahead and do it.

SCHEDULING TIME TO GAIN TIME

Lee Iacocca, president of Chrysler Corporation, who became internationally famous as the man who saved the company from almost certain bankruptcy in 1981, made this observation: "I'm constantly amazed by the number of people who can't seem to control their own schedules." The way we use time—or waste it—is largely a matter of habit. It is not easy to change old habits, but if they are bad habits, they put a ceiling on achievement. For example, a professional baseball player with a poor batting stance can become a good hitter, up to a point. Unless he improves his stance, however, progress behind that point is doubtful. To change and begin almost all over again—to break a bad habit and make a good one—takes determination and will, but the decision to change brings the chance for success. If you find that you need more time for all your studies and other activities, consider scheduling your time in order to gain time.

Where Does All the Time Go? _____

In an effort to find out specifically how he spent his time, a student kept a diary of his daily activities for one week. He found that his "ten-minute" coffee break was nearer forty minutes. Figure 1.2 shows one page of his diary and contains an analysis that demonstrates how the student could avoid dribbling away minutes and save hours for both recreation and study. A time log, or daily diary, is a valuable tool for getting control of time. Without a time log, you really don't know how you are spending your time. Try keeping one for a week or two.

Reasons for Scheduling _____

How much spare time do you have every day? The student whose activities record appears in Figure 1.2 would probably answer, "None. There are not enough hours in the day for all the things I have to do." That's the way things may seem to you too, but it's not necessarily the way they are.

Time Start	Time End	Time Used	Activity - Description
7:45	8:15	:30	Dress
8:15	8:40	:25	Breakfast
8:40	9:00	:20	Nothing
9:00	10:00	1:00	Psychology - Lecture
10:00	10:40	:40	Coffee - Talking
10:40	11:00	:20	Nothing
11:00	12:00	1:00	Economics - Lecture
12:00	12:45	:45	Lunch
12:45	2:00	1:15	Reading - Magazine
2:00	4:00	2:00	Biology Lab
4:00	5:30	1:30	Recreation - Volleyball
5:30	6:00	:30	Nothing
6:00	7:00	1:00	Dinner
7:00	8:00	1:00	Nap
8:00	8:50	:50	Study - Statistics
8:50	9:20	:30	Break
9:20	10:00	:40	Study - Statistics
10:00	10:50	:50	Chat with Bob
10:50	11:30	:40	Study - Accounting
11:30	11:45	:15	Ready for bed
11:45	7:45	8:00	Sleep.

Paste 3 X 5 cards on mirror: laws of economics; psychological terms; statistical formulas. Study while brushing teeth, etc.

Look over textbook assignment and previous lecture notes to establish continuity for today's psychology lecture.

Break too long and too soon after breakfast. Work on psychology notes just taken; also look over economics assignment.

Rework the lecture notes on economics while still fresh in mind. Also, look over biology assignment to recall the objective of the coming lab.

Use this time to read a magazine or newspaper.

Not a good idea. Better finish work, then get a good night's sleep.

Break is too long.

Good as a reward if basic work is done.

Insufficient time allotted, but better than no time.

While brushing teeth, study the 3 X 5 cards. Replace cards that have been mastered with new ones.

FIGURE 1.2 Record of One Day's Activities and Suggestions for Making Better Use of Time

TABLE 1.1 Time Spent by Students in a Typical Week

Activity	Hours Spent
Sleep	49.3
Study	19.8
Classes and labs	18.7
Meals	10.7
Total	98.5

Source: From "College Students Report on the Use of Time," by Arthur A. Dole in *The Personnel and Guidance Journal* 37 (May 1959), p. 635. Reprinted by permission of American Association for Counseling & Development.

Table 1.1 shows how students at one university spent time in four main activities during a typical week. The students spent 98.5 hours sleeping, studying, attending classes and labs, and eating their meals. When you subtract that total from 168 (the number of hours in a week), you have 69.5 hours unaccounted for—almost ten hours a day.

You can gain extra time in only two ways: (1) by doing a job in less time than usual, (2) by using small blocks of time that you usually waste. The first way requires you to study more efficiently, and this book provides a great many techniques to help you do just that. The second way requires you to schedule your time, and this chapter offers a number of suggestions.

Although some people believe it's a waste of time to make a schedule, planning actually *saves* time and energy. Sure, it takes time to schedule your time, but the time you spend making a schedule is returned to you several times over when you work—and relax—according to your schedule. Spending a little time to make a schedule saves a lot of time that you would otherwise waste.

Some people feel that maintaining a schedule will make robots or slaves of them. Just the opposite is true. The people you see dashing madly from class to library to gym, or eating a junk-food lunch on the run, are slaves to time because they are not in control of their time. The student who schedules time, who decides how it will be used, is the master of time rather than its slave.

Some people won't schedule their time because they want to be "flexible." But a disorganized person wastes so much time that there really isn't any time left to be flexible with. Scheduling, however, frees up time for a variety of activities, and flexibility can certainly be built into a schedule.

Scheduling actually gives you more time, makes you the master of your time, and provides the flexibility that *you* want. Here are some additional benefits of scheduling.

1. *Gets you started.*   You know how hard it is to get started. Often a well-planned schedule can be the external force that gives you a needed shove.

2. *Prevents avoidance of disliked subjects.*   The mind can play tricks. Without actually deciding to do so, you can keep yourself from doing something you don't like by occupying yourself with favorite subjects.

3. *Monitors the slackening-off process.*   By apportioning time properly, you can keep yourself from slackening off as the semester wears on.

4. *Eliminates the wrong type of cramming.*   If cramming just before exams is to be effective, the original studying and learning must take place day by day.

5. *Makes studying enjoyable.*   When done without the pressure of time, studying and learning can be intensely interesting.

6. *Promotes cumulative review.*   Sandwiching in short review periods is the best way to retain knowledge as well as to prepare for exams. It is less fatiguing and more effective to review a subject in four *distributed* thirty-minute sessions than in a single *massed* two-hour session.

7. *Frees the mind.*   To keep from forgetting details, you may think and rethink them. This often leads to a tense feeling of pressure and confusion. Putting things to do on paper takes them off the mental treadmill.

8. *Controls the study break.*   Rewarding yourself with a ten-minute break when you finish a scheduled block of study helps minimize clock watching. During short breaks, stand up, walk around, or just stare out the window, but keep in mind the subject you're studying. Then you won't need a warm-up period when you resume studying.

9. *Keeps you from overlooking recreation.*   Physical and social activities are needed for a well-balanced personality, good health, and efficient study. On the other hand, allowing extracurricular activities to outweigh studies probably accounts for more failures in college than anything else.

10. *Helps raise your recreational efficiency.*   One of the saddest wastes of time and pleasure is to mix study time and recreation time—that is, when studying, to keep thinking how nice it would be to be playing some game; and when playing, to think about all the studying that needs to be done.

11. *Regulates daily living.*   Without a plan to guide you, assignments are bound to pile up. When they do, you lose control, and your daily living

is thrown into chaos. With a schedule, even weekends and holidays can be free from worry.

PRINCIPLES OF SCHEDULING

Just as there are basic rules for driving a car, no matter how long or short a trip you are taking, so there are basic rules for making a study schedule. The following list includes general principles that apply to all study schedules.

1. *Eliminate dead hours.*   Make each block of one hour a productive unit. Some of the most important lessons of our lives are learned in less time.

2. *Use daylight hours.*   Research shows that each hour used for study during the day is equal to one and a half hours at night.

3. *Study before recitation-type classes.*   For a course in which you recite and discuss, it is an advantage to study just before class. The material will be fresh in your mind.

4. *Study after lecture-type classes.*   For a lecture course, retention and understanding are aided by a review of your lecture notes immediately after class.

5. *List according to priorities.*   By putting first things first, you are sure to get the most important things done on time.

6. *Avoid too much detail.*   Packing a weekly schedule with too many details is a waste of time for two reasons. The time you take to make such a schedule could be better used in studying a subject directly. The chances of your following such a schedule are very slim.

7. *Know your sleep pattern.*   We all have daily cycles of sleepiness and alertness. If your work, classes, and circumstances permit, sleep when you're sleepy and study when you're naturally alert.

8. *Discover how long to study.*   The rule of thumb that you should study two hours for every hour in class is a rough guide at best. The time required varies from student to student and from subject to subject. Start out allowing two hours of study for every hour in class, but adjust the hours according to your experience, as you find out how long you need to master each assignment.

9. *Plan blocks of time.*   Optimum efficiency is reached by planning in blocks of one hour: fifty minutes to study and ten minutes for a break.

10. *Allow time for sleep.*   Your need for eight hours of sleep every night is supported by medical evidence. Make no mistake about it: The quality of your education depends on sufficient sleep.

11. *Eat well-balanced meals.*   Take time for good meals. Living on greasy foods or a low-protein diet most of the time is no way to treat your body and brain. Dietary deficiencies result in irritability, fatigue, and lack of pep.

12. *Double your time estimates, and start long jobs ahead of time.*   Most people tend to underestimate the amount of time they need for a project. To avoid discovering the hard way that you cannot bang out a 1500-word paper in three hours the evening before it is due, start ridiculously early, thus allowing yourself more time.

13. *Don't pack your schedule too tightly.*   Be precise, but leave room for last-minute problems that require your time.

14. *Make a plan for living, not merely for studying.*   After all, life, even in college, is many-sided, and its many sides must be recognized.

TYPES OF SCHEDULES

It is important to choose the type of schedule that fits your circumstances best. Some students work best with a detailed schedule; others work best with a brief list of things to do. Circumstances also influence the type of schedule you should make. There are on-campus students, commuting students, married students, employed students, night-class students, and part-time students, and each has different scheduling requirements. You should *adapt* the principles of schedule building to your personal circumstances, rather than *adopt* some ideal model that fits hardly anybody, let alone you.

The schedule for *you* is the schedule that *works*. With time and experience, you can refine your schedule until it is an almost perfect fit for your situation.

Master Schedule

Any plan to schedule your time and activities must have at its core a master schedule—that is, a fixed schedule of activities. A master schedule needs to be drawn up only once each semester, unless changes occur in your basic program. Figure 1.3 shows a useful format.

First, fill in all required school activities, such as courses, classes, and laboratory periods. Then add other regular activities, such as a part-time job, commuting time, sports, and regular meetings. Next, add housekeeping chores, sleeping, and eating. When your fixed activities have been accounted for, the blank spaces on the chart are available for weekly or day-by-day planning. Here are some suggestions on how to use some of the time periods represented by the blank spaces in Figure 1.3.

	Mon.	Tues.	Wed.	Thurs.	Fri	Sat.	Sun.
7-8	←————Dress and Breakfast————→						
8-9	History		History		History	Dress + Breakfast	
9-10		Phy Ed		Phy Ed.		Phy Ed.	Dress + Breakfast
10-11		Chem		Chem.		Chem	
11-12	French		French		French		
12-1	←———————Lunch———————→						
1-2	Math	Film making	Math	Film making	Math		
2-3				↑			
3-4				Chem lab.			
4-5	English		English	↓	English		
5-6							
6-7	←———————Dinner———————→						
7-8							
8-9							
9-10							
10-11							
11-12	←———————Sleep———————→						

FIGURE 1.3   A Master Schedule

Monday/Wednesday/Friday

9–10 A.M.	Use the free period after history (a lecture course) to study lecture notes.
10–11	Since French (at 11) is a recitation course, prepare by studying during the free period that precedes class.
2–3 P.M.	In math class (1–2) problems are usually discussed and worked out on the blackboard. Take very brief notes on both discussion and blackboard work. Then, because math problems can quickly become "cold," use the free period (2–3) to go over the work covered in class during the preceding hour.
3–4	English (4–5) is often a discussion period. Use the free hour to study and warm up in advance.
7–8	Evening study time begins. Start with English, your last class, so that any notes you have taken can be reviewed before forgetting takes place.
8–9	Study French, giving priority to the notes and assignments of the day.

Such a master schedule, on a 5 × 8 card taped over your desk or carried in your notebook, unclutters your mind. More important, it enables you to visualize the blank boxes as actual blocks of time into which you may fit necessary activities. With the master schedule as your base, you can devise any type of schedule that fits your unique combination of courses, your part-time or full-time job, and your personality.

Detailed Weekly Schedule

Some people work best when they are guided by a weekly schedule that is an expansion of the master schedule. If the demands on your time are both heavy and predictable, you may need a detailed weekly schedule. This kind of schedule needs to be made out only once, early in the semester. A sample weekly schedule is shown in Figure 1.4. The lists that follow indicate how the principles of scheduling were used to set it up.

Monday Through Friday/Saturday

7–8 A.M.	Avoid the frantic dash and the gobbled (or skipped) breakfast by getting up on time.
12–1 P.M.	Take a full, leisurely hour for lunch.
5–6	Relax before dinner—your reward for a day of conscientious work.

Time	Mon.	Tues.	Wed.	Thurs.	Fri.	Sat.	Sun.
7-8	←———— Dress and Breakfast ————→						↑
8-9	History	Study Chem.	History	Study Chem.	History	Study Chem.	
9-10	Study History	Phy. Ed.	Study History	Phy. Ed.	Study History	Phy. Ed.	
10-11	Study French	Chem.	Study French	Chem.	Study French	Chem.	Church, Recreation, Conversation, Recreational Reading
11-12	French	Study Chem.	French	Study Chem.	French	Study Chem.	
12-1	←———— Lunch ————→						
1-2	Math	Film-making	Math	Film-making	Math		
2-3	Study Math	Library: Paper	Study Math	↑	Study Math	Special Projects, Conversation on Difficult Subjects	
3-4	Study English	"	Study English	Chem. Lab.	Study English		
4-5	English	"	English	↓	English		
5-6	←———— Recreation ————→						
6-7	←———— Dinner ————→						↓
7-8	Study English	Study Math	Study English	Study Math	Study English	Recreation, Conversation, Reading; Extra Work on Difficult Subjects; Thorough Review.	English Paper
8-9	Study French	Study History	Study French	Study History	Study French		English Paper
9-10	Review English	Review French	Review History	Review Math	Review Chem.		Study History
10-11	←———— Recreational Reading ————→						
11-12	←———— Conversation, Sleep ————→						↓

FIGURE 1.4   A Detailed Weekly Schedule Based on a Master Schedule

7–9	Keep up with current notes and assignments by systematic studying.
9–10	To forestall cramming at quiz and examination times, give some time every day to a review of previous assignments and ground covered to date.
10	A cease-study time of 10 P.M. is an incentive to work hard during the day and early evening.
10–12	Devote some time every day to reading books that truly interest you. Recreational reading and conversation help you unwind for a good night's sleep.

Tuesday/Thursday/Saturday

8–9 A.M.	Since chemistry (10–11) is your hard subject, build your morning study program around it. An hour's study before class will make the class period more meaningful.
11–12	Another hour's study immediately after chemistry class will help you remember the work covered in class and move more readily to the next assignment.

Special

Tuesday	2–5 P.M., library: paper
Sunday	7–9 P.M., English paper
	For some assignments you will need to schedule blocks of time to do research or to develop and follow up ideas.
Saturday	From noon on, Saturday is left unscheduled—for recreation, for special projects to which you must devote a concentrated period of time, for extra work on difficult subjects, for thorough review.
Sunday	This is your day until evening. Study history before you go to bed, because it is the first class you'll have on Monday morning.

Assignment-oriented Weekly Schedule _____

Another type of weekly schedule is based primarily on assignments, rather than on available time. It is a supplement to the master schedule and can be used whenever you face unusual or long-term assignments. Because it schedules specific assignments, it covers only one specific week.

Figure 1.5 shows a weekly assignment schedule. The format is simple: Draw a horizontal line to divide a lined sheet of paper approximately in half. In the top half list your subjects, assignments, estimated study times, and due

Subject	Assignment	Estimated Time	Date Due	Time Due
Electronics	Chap. I - 32 pp. - Read	2 hr.	Mon. 13th	8:00
English	Paper to Write	18 hr.	Mon. 20th	9:00
Math	Problems on pp. 110-111	3 hr.	Tues. 14th	10:00
Industrial Safety	Make shop layouts	8 hr.	Fri. 17th	11:00
Graphics	Drawing of TV components	6 hr.	Fri. 17th	1:00
Electronics	Chap. II - 40 pp. - Read	2½ hr.	Weds. 22nd	8:00

Day	Assignment	Morning	Afternoon	Evening
Sun.	Electronics - Read Chap. I English - Find a Topic			7:30- 9:30 9:30-10:30
Mon	English - Gather Notes Math - Problems		2:00 - 6:00	7:00-10:00
Tues	English - Gather Notes Industrial Safety	8:00-10:00	3:00 - 6:00	7:00 -10:00
Wed.	English - First Draft Graphics		2:00 - 6:00	7:00- 10:00
Thurs	Industrial Safety English- Paper Graphics	8:00 - 10:00	3:00- 6:00	7:00-10:00
Fri	English - Final Copy Electronics		2:00 - 6:00	7:00 - 9:30
Sat				

FIGURE 1.5 A Weekly Schedule Based on Assignments
To provide a time dimension, this schedule is being made out on Saturday, November 11, for the coming week.

dates. Then, using the due dates and estimated times as control factors, check your master schedule for hours available. Choose enough hours to do each job, and write them on the appropriate line on the bottom half of the weekly schedule sheet. *Stick to your schedule.* Give study hours top priority. As long as you do, your remaining free hours will be really free.

FOR MONDAY

8 - 9	Psychology - Review Chapter V and lecture notes
9 - 10	Psychology lecture
10 - 11	Economics lecture
11 - 12	Economics - fix up notes, begin Chapter III
1 - 2	Campus store - Pick up paper and binder, pen, lead, calculator
2 - 5	Engineering - work on assignment
5 - 6	Exercise - Tennis court with Joan.
7 - 10	Accounting and Math

Review: Just before class is a good time to review the high points of chapters previously studied. Also review the previous lecture for continuity.

Fix up notes: The very best time to fix up lecture notes, and review them simultaneously, is immediately after the lecture.

After lunch: This is a good time to give yourself a semi-break from academic work and do some necessary errands.

2-5 block: This is a valuable block of time during which you should be able to read the assignment and work out the assigned problems without losing continuity.

Exercise: After an entire day with the books, some exercise and a shower will help to put an edge on your appetite, as well as making a definite break between study during the day and study during the evening.

Breaks: Breaks are not listed. You judge for yourself when a break is best for you. Also, the break should be taken when you arrive at a good stopping point.

After dinner: Both subjects need unbroken time for efficient production. Use the block of three hours to do a balanced amount of work for each, depending on the assignments.

FIGURE 1.6 A Daily Schedule

Daily Schedule

You will probably want to have a daily schedule that you can carry around with you. A 3 × 5 card is just the right size. It will fit perfectly into your shirt pocket or shoulder bag and will be at hand when you need it. Every evening before leaving your desk, look at your master schedule to determine your free hours and courses for the next day. Then jot down on the card a plan for the next day: the subjects you plan to study, the errands, appointments, physical exercise, recreation, and any other activities you want to do, and the time you allot for each. The five minutes you spend are important for two reasons. First, you will have a written record to which you can refer, and this will unclutter your mind. Second, you will have mentally thought through your day, thus putting into action a psychological clock that will help keep you on schedule.

Notice in Figure 1.6 that the daily schedule is organized on the basis of blocks of time, rather than fragments of time. By assigning a block of time to each topic or activity, you will ensure that you work at peak efficiency.

Scheduling Long-Term Assignments _____

Most assignments are not portioned out in bite-size, day-by-day units. Some assignments span a week, some a month, some (research papers and projects) an entire semester. Although it pays to study every day, you must also do some long-term planning.

You are likely to have one or two long-term assignments at all times, and you may get confused if you have too many separate schedules. It is best to keep a record of the full assignments and their due dates in your notebook for each subject. Get started on these assignments early by allotting some time to each of them on your daily schedules. If you still have trouble remembering to do them, you may need to make out a weekly assignment schedule like the one shown in Figure 1.5.

SCHEDULING FOR STUDENTS WITH JOBS

If you have a full-time or part-time job, you probably have less time and less energy for studying than regular full-time students; consequently, you must use your time and energy very carefully. A full-time student can use big blocks of uninterrupted time for studying, but you must find ways to use scattered pieces of time.

If you are a working student, your daily study schedule should simply be a list of things to do, in the order of priority. Figure 1.7 shows a typical daily list for a working student. To be successful, you should have a sense of urgency about referring to your list and studying whenever an opportunity presents itself. Cross off the tasks you complete. Assigning specific times is likely to lead only to frustration. Your study materials should be in a form that permits you to carry them about for use whenever you have some spare time.

Preparing Notes for Study on the Run _____

To take advantage of moments of spare time, your study materials must be readily available. One way to make them available is to write or type notes on small cards; another way is to record notes on cassettes.

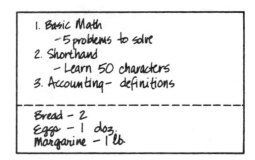

1. Basic Math
   - 5 problems to solve
2. Shorthand
   - Learn 50 characters
3. Accounting - definitions

Bread - 2
Eggs - 1 doz.
Margarine - 1 lb.

FIGURE 1.7　A Things-to-Do Schedule for a Working Student

After reading an assignment or attending a lecture, select from it only the information that you believe is important enough to master. Using your own words, write or type this information on 3 × 5 or 5 × 8 cards. You can then record the same notes, or a portion of them, on cassettes. If you have time for only one of these, use the cards.

How to Study on the Run

Here are some ways to study during time periods that are ordinarily only half-used.

1. Attach small metal or plastic clips near mirrors and on walls, at eye level. Place a note card in each clip. While shaving or combing your hair, or while washing dishes, you can read the notes on the cards. Cards placed in clips can be easily changed; pasting or taping cards to walls is not as practical.

2. To vary the routine and to use your sense of hearing, listen to a cassette or two while going through your morning routine.

3. When you drive to work, listen to several cassettes instead of to music on the car radio. If you have only cards, recite aloud from memory (not verbatim) some of the ideas, formulas, or definitions that are on the cards. After you stop driving, read the cards to check your accuracy.

4. As you walk from the parking lot to your place of work, flip through several of your note cards or listen to a cassette.

5. At lunch, while eating a sandwich in your place of work, do a problem or two in math, or, if you prefer, listen to a cassette.

Knowing how to study on the run will enable you to devote more time to your family, job, and school without scrimping on sleep.

TIPS FOR SAVING TIME

You have twenty-four hours of time every day. You get no more and no less, whether you're rich or poor, stingy or spendthrift, deserving or undeserving. You cannot buy or manufacture more time. There are, however, three ways to accomplish more within the hours you have: (1) by using the mini-size study skills explained in this section; (2) by using the self-discipline strategies explained in this section; and (3) by using the time you once wasted.

Mini-Size Study Skills

Bundle-of-Sticks Technique. A father once tied a bundle of small, thin sticks together with a strand of twine. Handing the bundle to his youngest son, he said, "Son, break these sticks in half." The boy used his hands and knees but could not break the bundle. Sadly, he handed it back to his father. Without a word, the father untied the twine and, using only his fingers, snapped each stick, one by one.

When one of your assignments is long and seems overwhelming, unbundle it and divide it into small, manageable units—units that you can start on immediately. For example, when you're assigned a research paper to write, spring into action immediately by breaking the assignment into small, practical units, and do one or two of them per day:

1. Choose a topic. Remind yourself to choose a topic in which you are interested.

2. Narrow the topic; in fact, make three or four significant narrowings.

3. Look in the *Readers' Guide to Periodical Literature* to see how much current information there is on your topic.

4. Sharpen the focus of the topic to make sure you are answering a question.

5. Buy a stack of 3 × 5 cards or slips of paper for recording your bibliography and notes.

6. Look in the card catalogue, and make bibliographical notes.

7. Look in the reference sections, and make notes.

8. Look in the periodical sections, and make notes.

9. Take separate notes for the bibliography and for detailed information for your paper.

10. Etc. (For more detailed information on researching and writing papers, see Chapter 18 of Pauk: *How to Study in College*, or follow the steps described in any good book on writing papers.)

Right from the beginning, remind yourself that you do not intend to plunge into the main job of writing the paper. After you have divided the assignment, begin your work in the first free study period of the same day, while the full concept is still fresh in your mind. Once underway, the paper will practically write itself.

The secret of the Bundle-of-Sticks Technique is to make the pieces the right size so that each is easy to do. "Divide and conquer" applies to assignments just as it does to military tactics.

Setting a Time Limit for Each Task.   According to Parkinson's Law: Work expands to fill the time available for its completion.[1] To be sure you don't run out of time before you've finished a project, work Parkinson's Law in reverse: For each task, set a deadline that you will find difficult to meet, and then work hard to meet that deadline.

Each time you achieve your goal, reward yourself with a pleasant activity (any behavior that is followed by something pleasant tends to be reinforced and is more likely to happen again). Take a break. Briefly chat with a friend. Get a drink of water. Walk around the room. You may want to keep a special snack, such as a jar of peanuts, in the bottom drawer of your desk, to be opened only as a reward. Lee Iacocca used this principle in college and even as a child:

> As a little kid I had learned how to do my homework right after school so that I could play after supper. By the time I got to college, . . . I used to tell myself: "I'm going to give this my best shot for the next three hours. And when those three hours are up, I'll set this work aside and go to the movies."[2]

Remember these two additional principles:

1. If you fail to meet a deadline, don't punish yourself harshly by, for example, not going to a football game. Your punishment is sufficient if you deprive yourself of the peanuts in your desk. It is *positive* reinforcement that is powerful in effecting a change in behavior.

2. Reward yourself for your small successes, not only for your major ones.

The Pareto Principle.[3]   Named after Vilfredo Pareto (1848–1923), an Italian economist and sociologist, the Pareto Principle states that the truly

---

[1]C. Northcote Parkinson, *Parkinson's Law and Other Studies in Administration* (Boston: Houghton Mifflin, 1957).
[2]Lee Iacocca, with William Novak, *Iacocca: An Autobiography* (New York: Bantam Books, 1984), p. 20.
[3]Reprinted by permission of Charles Scribner's Sons, an imprint of Macmillan Publishing Company and Macdonald & Co. Publishers Ltd. from *Getting Things Done: The ABC's of Time Management* by Edwin C. Bliss. Copyright © 1976 Edwin C. Bliss.

important items in any given group constitute only a small number of the total items in that group. This principle is also known as the 80/20 rule.

For example, in almost any sales force, 80 percent of the business is brought in by 20 percent of the salespeople. In any committee, 80 percent of the ideas come from 20 percent of the members. In a classroom, 80 percent of the teacher's time is taken up by 20 percent of the students.

In any list of things to do, 80 percent of the importance resides in 20 percent of the list. In a list of ten items, 80 percent of the list's value lies in 2 items, which constitute 20 percent of the list. Because of Pareto's Principle, in your lists of things to do always put the most important items first. Then, if you accomplish only the first few items, you will have accomplished the most important tasks on the list.

Keep the Pareto Principle in mind whenever you make up a list or a schedule or must decide which subject to study first. Apply the principle by listing first things first.

Concentrating Your Time and Efforts.   Some students jump from subject to subject when they study, scattering their time and efforts. They touch many assignments but finish none. When you focus the sun's rays onto a piece of paper, the rays will burn a hole; unfocused rays, like scattered time and effort, make no impression at all. Pause, make a plan, and then take action. Remember that action without planning won't get you very far.

Planning Ahead.   You must not try to play things by ear. No football coach would field a team without a game plan, and no student should try to face a school day without an academic game plan. If you do not have one, other people's actions will determine what you do, and your time will be wasted. By having a plan of your own, you will be able to use your time to achieve *your* goals.

Using a Month-at-a-Glance Calendar.   Buy or make—but use—a calendar that shows the entire month on one page. For precise control, you need to see what assignments are due and when at a glance. A page per week won't do. Above all, don't use a page for each day, because assignments hidden from view in next week's pages are out of sight and out of mind.

Taking Study Breaks.   Which is better: sticking with a two-hour assignment until you have finished it or breaking the assignment into half-hour periods separated by five-minute breaks? Breaking up a long assignment is better, for several reasons:

1. Study breaks keep you from getting tired and bored.
2. You work harder and concentrate better in short spurts.

3. Five-minute breaks are great motivators.

4. During the rest periods, the material you studied has a chance to sink in.

However, just as some runners need a long time to warm up, some students take a long time to get into a long assignment. If such students broke long assignments into half-hour periods, they would need warming up at the end of every half hour. Such students should study for a full fifty minutes or longer before taking a ten-minute break. It is better for them to be like marathon runners, finishing the long assignment in one continuous stretch.

Before you take a break, review your underlinings and jottings. This will help the facts sink into your long-term memory. Just before a break is also a good time to reread a particularly difficult problem or passage. This gets your mind working on the problem while you rest.

Beating the Sleepy Feeling.   While studying, if you get sleepy before your scheduled sleep time, *don't* take a nap. Instead, pick up your textbook, stand up, and pace the floor, reading aloud as you do. The sleepy feeling will pass. When you go to bed at your scheduled time, you'll be able to fall asleep.

Writing Notes to Yourself.   When you reach the end of a study session, write a note telling yourself where to begin during your next study period. You'll be surprised at how much time this practice will save you each day, and you'll enjoy the boost that such a note provides.

Self-Discipline Strategies

A "yes" answer to any of the following questions is a sure sign of poor planning and poor self-discipline:

1. Did you have to cram for an exam?

2. Did you have to stay up most of the night to finish a term or research paper?

3. Did you have to give up your recreational time?

4. Did you have to miss a basketball or a football game in order to study?

5. Did you have to excuse yourself from going to a good movie with friends?

If you answered "yes" to any of them, take out a sheet of paper and write down why you had this problem; then list specific ways that you could have avoided the problem and ways that you can prevent it from happening again. By taking this action, you show that you are in control of your life.

Here are some other strategies to bolster your self-discipline.

Deciding to Change Your Behavior.   Old habits are difficult to break and new ones difficult to make, but you can do it if you follow these rules:

1. *Develop a strong determination.*   If you want to make or break a habit, your determination must be powerful enough to carry you over rough spots. Every day you succeed, the success of your plan is made more certain.

2. *Never, ever make an exception.*   Making an exception is like dropping a carefully wound ball of string: "A single slip undoes more than a great many turns will wind again."[4] Never willingly lose a battle.

3. *Take every opportunity to put your good habit to work.*   Always practice behavior that you want to come naturally.

Listing Tasks According to Their Importance.   Do you list your priorities according to importance or according to urgency? Should tomorrow's quiz head your list, or should you do some work on that long-range research paper that could make or break your final grade? If your priority lists reflect urgency instead of importance, you have a problem: You began working on such tasks too late, and as time runs out, you must rush frantically to meet your deadline. As a result, you shove aside your heavyweight research paper to make room for a quiz. Avoid this situation. Start early, and work steadily.

Understanding the Relationship Between Time and Goals.   There is a direct relationship between goals and time. When you have a goal firmly in mind, you will think of objectives rather than activities. You will make better decisions, speak and write more forcefully, and treat time as a precious commodity. You will be as serious about time as Ben Franklin, who said, "Time is the stuff of which life is made," and you will avoid falling victim to the four great robbers of time:

1. Laziness: "I don't feel like doing it now."
2. Sidetracks: "I'll wash my hair and then I'll begin working."
3. Procrastination: "Sure, I'll do it later."
4. Daydreaming: "Some day I'll amaze them."

Concentrating on One Task at a Time.   Nothing can help you use time more productively than concentration. Many students never become proficient concentrators because they try to do too many things at once. All your

---

[4]William James, *Psychology* (New York: Holt, 1893), p. 145.

tasks may be important, but you can do only one at a time. To start the time-saving process, you must decide which one task is most important. Push all else aside. Set a realistic deadline, and then work on this task until you have completed it. When you have finished, reward yourself with a five-minute break.

Avoiding Procrastination.   "Nothing [is] so fatiguing as the eternal hanging on of an uncompleted task."[5] These words by William James (1842–1910), distinguished American psychologist, strike at the heart of us all. Every one of us has had many bouts with procrastination.

If a task that you are doing is about three-quarters finished and is finishable, finish it no matter how tired you are. If you delay completion until tomorrow, you'll need extra time to overcome inertia, reread what you have done, pick up your train of thought, and recapture yesterday's momentum.

Make it a habit to save both time and energy by doing a needed task immediately or at the first free opportunity. By doing so, you prove that you are in control of your life.

Obeying the Alarm Clock.   Once you have decided on a time to get up, don't ignore the decision when the alarm goes off. Without stretching, yawning, or groaning, make your feet hit the floor immediately. Five minutes later, you'll be glad you did.

Striving for Excellence.   In *Getting Things Done,* Edwin C. Bliss writes: "There is a difference between striving for excellence and striving for perfection. The first is attainable, gratifying, and healthy. The second is unattainable and frustrating. It's also a terrible waste of time."[6] If you strive for perfection, you will waste time and energy that you could put to good use elsewhere. Trivial errors in your papers, for example, could be corrected neatly in ink; they do not necessitate retyping. In sum, do the best you can; then go on to the next task.

Acknowledging That Everyone Makes Mistakes.   Because we all make many errors in judgment, the words "Everyone makes mistakes" help us preserve our self-image and self-confidence and keep us from giving up on ourselves. Do not use this expression to excuse mistakes that were easily avoidable, however. Try to understand how and why you erred so that you can prevent a reoccurrence. Once you have come to terms with a mistake, put it

---

[5]William James, *The Selected Letters of William James.* Ed. with an introduction by Elizabeth Hardwick (New York: Farrar, Straus & Cudahy, 1960, 1961), p. 125.
[6]Bliss, p. 79.

behind you and concentrate on using the precious minutes of today for today's living.

Having Courage. You need personal courage to follow a good schedule because when you do so, you'll leave some students behind—perhaps some who are your friends. You may feel some loneliness, but you can take pride in the fact that you are controlling your life and achieving your goals.

Using Time Once Wasted

Getting a Head Start. If possible, finalize your class schedule before classes start, so that you can plan the days and weeks that lie ahead. Buy your textbooks early, before the campus store runs out of stock. Being without a textbook for even a little while can throw your study schedule off-balance. Before the first session of each class, visit the building and room where the class is to be held, so that you will know exactly where to go on the hectic, first day.

Carrying Pocket Work. Always carry some work you can do while you are waiting in lines and in places such as bus stations and air terminals, while you are sitting down to rest, while you are eating alone, and so forth. Never be without pocket work such as 3 × 5 cards carrying key words, key concepts, or formulas; a few pages photocopied from an important part of your textbook; or a paperback book. Also carry a few blank cards for jotting down brilliant ideas that occur to you.

Spare-Time Thinking. Use your spare time to think. While you're walking *from* a class, try to recall the main points of the lecture you just heard. If you're walking *to* a class, try to recall the main points of the lecture you heard at the last meeting of the class. At other times—when you're jogging, for example—try to think up interesting topics and titles for your next paper.

Using Your Subconscious. At one time or another, you have awakened during the night with a bright idea or a solution to a problem that you had been thinking about before bedtime. Your subconscious works while your conscious mind is resting in sleep. If you want to capture the ideas or solutions produced by your subconscious, you should write them down as soon as you wake up; otherwise, they'll be lost. Many creative people know this and keep a pad and pencil near their beds. For example, Nobel Prize winner Albert Szent-Györgyi said, "I go to sleep thinking about my problems all the time, and my brain must continue to think about them when I sleep because

I wake up, sometimes in the middle of the night, with answers to questions that have been eluding me all day."[7]

At Stanford University, Dr. William Dement and his colleagues studied the phenomenon of problem solving in dreams. Five hundred students were given the following two problems to solve at two different and separate times. Try to solve these problems before looking at the answers that follow.

Problem 1: The letters O,T,T,F,F . . . form the beginning of an infinite sequence. Find a simple rule for determining any or all successive letters. According to your rule, what would be the next two letters of the sequence?

Problem 2: Consider the letters H,I,J,K,L,M,N,O. The solution to this problem is one word. What is this word?[8]

The students were instructed to read the problem fifteen minutes before going to bed. The correct solutions appeared in the dreams of nine students.

In Problem 1, the letters in the sequence are the first letters of *one, two, three, four,* and *five.* The next two letters in the sequence are therefore S, S.

In Problem 2, the solution is the word *water.* The sequence of letters runs from *H* to *O,* and H_2O is the chemical formula for water.

Working During Prime Time.   There's a certain time of day when you do most of your best work. If you work best from 6 to 8 A.M., set up an early-to-bed and early-to-rise schedule. Remember to schedule your one or two highest-priority assignments for your prime time. Work on other assignments at other times.

GETTING THINGS DONE

A schedule represents a plan. Just as the buzz of an alarm clock is a signal to get up, so sitting down at your desk should be a signal to begin to study. If you make a habit of getting started immediately and then studying vigorously, you will accomplish a great deal, and your feeling of satisfaction will make it easy for you to get started next time.

This vigorous, aggressive approach must become your way of life in the classroom, the laboratory, the library, and elsewhere. Get what you came for! During a lecture, for example, be alert and work hard to capture the lecturer's ideas and get them down on paper.

---

[7]Originally published in SOME MUST WATCH WHILE SOME MUST SLEEP by William C. Dement as a volume in The Portable Stanford series published by the Stanford Alumni Association. Copyright © 1972. Reprinted by permission of the Stanford Alumni Association.
[8]Ibid., pp. 99–100.

In the library, some students wander aimlessly or spend most of their time looking around and watching other students coming and going. If your purpose is to gather data for your research paper, then go to the card catalogue, gather your references, find the books, begin reading and taking notes. Get something done according to plan.

The intelligent use of time is a large part of academic success. Schedule your time wisely, and be sure to follow your plan.

SUMMARY

What's the number-one skill that I need to master in college?

Time management heads the list of skills that you need to learn. It can mean the difference between success and failure in college.

Where does all the time go? I don't feel as though I'm wasting much time, yet I never seem to have enough.

Wasting time becomes such a habit that you don't realize you're wasting it. One excellent way to keep track of where your time goes is with a time log, in which you keep a precise record of how you spend your time, right down to the minute. If you're like most students, you'll be able to reclaim hours of wasted time.

Won't making a schedule consume more time than it saves?

Making a schedule is not busywork. Taking the time to write up a schedule is like making an investment but, unlike the case with most investments, the returns are almost guaranteed. If you spend a few minutes to draw up a schedule, you'll save far more time than you spent scheduling, you'll feel more relaxed, and you'll get more done.

What is the master schedule?

The master schedule is a day-by-day, hour-by-hour breakdown of your typical week. The master schedule should feature the immovables of your semester—the things that aren't going to change from week to week, such as meals, sleep, a job (if you have one), and classes. Once these "obligations" have been filled in, the master schedule should provide you with an excellent illustration of the time you have available.

What is the detailed weekly schedule?

The detailed weekly schedule picks up where the master schedule leaves off. In addition to showing your semester-long obligations, it shows how you intend to use each block of free time. To make a detailed weekly schedule, photocopy your master schedule several times and use it as the foundation for your weekly schedule.

How does the assignment-oriented weekly schedule differ from the detailed weekly schedule?

Instead of being divided up by blocks of time, the assignment-oriented schedule is split into individual assignments. All the information it contains can fit on a single sheet of paper. The top half of the sheet contains a list of your assignments, the time you estimate that each will take, and the date and time due for each. The bottom half of the sheet contains the days of the week, along with the assignments, and splits each day into morning, afternoon, and evening. You write in the day you plan to work on the assignment and the time of day that you want to work on it.

What is the daily schedule?

The daily schedule can usually be squeezed onto a 3 × 5 card. It lists the things you plan to do each day and the time you plan to spend on each. A written record that you carry around with you is an excellent reminder and a great motivator.

How does scheduling differ for students who have jobs?

A working student must use time far more efficiently than a full-time student. Because working students lack the luxury of large blocks of free time, the daily schedule of a working student should simply be a list of things to do, ordered by priority but not limited by time. The tasks can then be crossed off the list whenever free time presents itself.

What is the mini-size study skill called the Bundle-of-Sticks Technique?

Just as a bundle of sticks is easy to break when you break one stick at a time, a large assignment becomes less threatening if you divide it into manageable tasks and work on each task separately.

Why should I set a time limit for my tasks?

The purpose of this mini-size study skill is to prevent you from spending too much time on any one aspect of a project. According to Parkinson's Law, work expands to fill the time available for its completion. You should reverse Parkinson's Law by setting deadlines that you will have difficulty meeting and then reward yourself for meeting them.

What is the Pareto Principle?

Also known as the 80/20 rule, the Pareto Principle tells us a very interesting fact about the tasks we set for ourselves. In any list of things to do, 80 percent of the list's value resides in 20 percent of the items on the list. What that means in concrete terms is that you need to identify the most important tasks to be accomplished. Following the Pareto Principle is a mini-size study skill that will prevent you from spending too much time on relatively unimportant tasks and ignoring the crucial ones.

Are study breaks a good idea?

They can be, and getting the most out of them is an enjoyable mini-size study skill. A short break—five minutes for every half hour of work—gives you a rest, allows you to work in short, efficient spurts, creates motivation that carries you over until the next break, and, most important, gives your brain some time to let new knowledge sink in.

Are there any little tricks of the trade that can help me save time?

Yes. There are five ways to use time that you once wasted. (1) *Get a head start.* Plan your class schedule, buy your books, and locate your classrooms in advance. That way, when the semester begins, you'll be spending time on work instead of on preparations. (2) *Carry pocket work.* If you have some work with you, while the rest of the world is waiting in line and getting more impatient by the minute, you'll be relaxing and accomplishing things as well. (3) *Think in your spare time.* Instead of daydreaming between classes, use that time for real thinking. If you're leaving a class, give some thought to the lecture you just heard. If you're on your way to a class, recall the key points from the last lecture. (4) *Use your subconscious.* Your subconscious is working even when you're asleep. If you wake up with an inspired idea, write it down instead of letting it slip away. (5) *Work during your prime time.* There is a time of day when you do your best work. Use that time to work on high-priority assignments.

HAVE YOU MISSED SOMETHING?

1. *Sentence completion.*   Complete the following sentences with one of the three words listed below each sentence.

    a.   In order to take control of your life, you must take control of your

    _____.

    personality   principles   time

    b.   How we spend or waste time is largely a matter of _____ .
         habit   procrastination   priority

2. *Matching.*   In each blank space in the left column, write the number preceding the phrase in the right column that matches the left item best.

    _____ a. Procrastination
    _____ b. Parkinson's Law
    _____ c. Pareto Principle
    _____ d. Perfection
    _____ e. Planning
    _____ f. Priorities

    1. A saver of time and energy
    2. Unattainable and frustrating goal
    3. One of the four great robbers of time
    4. Work expands to fill the time available for its completion
    5. Should reflect importance rather than urgency
    6. Also known as the 80/20 rule

3. *True-false.* Write *T* beside the *true* statements and *F* beside the *false* statements.

_____ a. The master schedule should be updated daily.

_____ b. It's best to study notes from a lecture course immediately after class.

_____ c. A leisurely breakfast can start a productive day.

_____ d. Your goal will be the same whether you put it in writing or keep it in your head.

_____ e. A month-at-a-glance calendar is recommended for optimum time management.

_____ f. All assignments should be broken up into half-hour study sessions.

4. *Study breaks.* Write "yes" next to the advantages of study breaks.

_____ a. Prevent you from getting tired or bored

_____ b. Give you a chance to take a refreshing nap

_____ c. Help you work harder and concentrate better

_____ d. Divide hour-long study sessions into four or five bite-sized pieces

_____ e. Provide motivation during the work period

_____ f. Allow work to sink in

5. *Multiple choice.* Choose the phrase that completes the following sentence most accurately, and circle the letter that precedes it.

Of the three steps toward success, action is the

a. easiest to achieve but the most important.
b. hardest to achieve but the least important.
c. hardest to achieve as well as the most important.
d. easiest to achieve as well as the least important.

CHAPTER 2

Note Taking

"The horror of that moment," the King went on, "I shall never, never forget!" "You will, though," the Queen said, "if you don't make a memorandum of it."

Lewis Carroll, pen name of Charles Lutwidge Dodgson (1832–98), author of *Alice's Adventures in Wonderland*

The bright-eyed cub reporter in the old movies really knew what he was doing. He scribbled down facts and ideas in a pocket pad. Although notetaking techniques have changed since then, the reason for taking notes is the same as it's always been: Note taking helps information stick in your memory. Whether you're capturing the words of a world leader or a classroom lecturer, you need to take notes quickly and efficiently. This chapter gives you the scoop on proper note taking. It reports on

- The importance of notes
- Tips and tactics
- The Cornell Note-taking System
- Types of notes
- Combining textbook and lecture notes
and finally
- Abbreviations and symbols

Many students attribute their academic and professional success to what they learned from classroom lectures. This is not surprising because professors and instructors are at their best when they are teaching and inspiring through lecturing. If you expect to learn from lectures, you must take notes. You must, like the cub reporter of old, get the information down in black and white.

THE IMPORTANCE OF NOTES

Forgetting can be *instantaneous* and *complete*. Note taking is a vital skill in college because forgetting occurs so quickly and so thoroughly. Many experiments suggest that unless you mentally rehearse the information you receive, you are unlikely to retain it in your short-term memory for more than about twenty seconds.[1] Hermann Ebbinghaus, the German psychologist who investigated remembering and forgetting, found that almost half of what is learned is forgotten within an hour.[2] Recently, psychologists carrying out experiments similar to Ebbinghaus' confirmed his findings.

The following true story further confirms the rapidity and massiveness of forgetting. Three professors eating lunch in the faculty lounge had this conversation:

CLYDE: Did you hear last night's lecture?
WALTER: No, I was busy.
CLYDE: Well, you missed one of the best lectures in recent years.
LEON: I agree. The four points that he developed were gems.
CLYDE: I never heard anyone make his points so clear.
WALTER: I don't want you to repeat the lecture, but what were those four points?
LEON: (Long silence) Clyde? (Passage of two or three minutes; seems like an hour.)
LEON: Well, I'd better get back to the office.
CLYDE: Me too!
WALTER: Me too!

Neither Leon nor Clyde was able to recall even a fragment of any point made in the previous night's lecture. Each of them forgot the four points because neither of them had transferred the points from short-term memory to long-term memory by silently reciting them. Instead, they both had recited

---

[1] Douglas A. Bernstein, Edward J. Roy, Thomas K. Srull, and Christopher D.Wickens, *Psychology* (Boston: Houghton Mifflin, 1988), p. 293.

[2] Hermann Ebbinghaus, *Memory.* Translated by Henry A. Ruger and Clara E. Bussenius (New York: Dover Publications, 1964 [1913]), p. 76.

that the speaker was clear, forceful, and wise, and that he had made four points—and they remembered only what they had recited.

The only sure way to overcome forgetting is by taking notes, then taking your notes back to your room to study and recite.

TIPS AND TACTICS

If you turn these tips and tactics into habits, your notes will be the envy of your classmates. Use these tips and tactics until they are second nature to you.

Telegraphic Sentences

Sixty years ago, when telephones were not so numerous as they are to-day, important messages, both personal and business, were sent by telegraph. The sender paid by the word; so the fewer the words, the lower was the cost. A four-word message such as "Will arrive three pm" was a lot less expensive than an eleven-word message: "I will arrive home promptly at 3 o'clock in the afternoon."

When you take notes, use telegraphic sentences. Leave out unnecessary words. Use the key words only. Ignore rules of grammar. Write down a streamlined version of the lecturer's key points. Two examples of the telegraphic style are given in Figure 2.1.

Modified Printing Style

Terrible handwriting need not prevent you from taking legible notes. You can give up your old way of writing and adopt the modified printing style. Your writing will be surprisingly rapid and amazingly clear. Anyone can adopt this style and use it to write neatly and clearly.

Here is how the individual letters look in the modified printing style:

a b c d e f g h i j k l m n o p q r s t u v w x y z

If you have your own way of forming some of the letters, use it. What flows naturally from your pen or pencil will be swifter and easier than a forced change. Figure 2.2 shows the style used in a paragraph.

In selling, you can overcome a customer's objections to almost any product if you can come up with a good idea. Here are two examples: first, a lady who objected to a square flyswatter bought it when the sales manager said, "These are square, madam. They get them in the corners." Second, a lady who wanted round clothespins, bought the square ones when the clerk said, "They don't roll out of reach under a sink." So, don't sell the steak - sell the sizzle.

Student's telegraphic sentences

1. *People buy ideas, not products.*
   a. *Ex. square flyswatter = "get in corners."*
   b. *Ex. square clothespins = "won't roll - sink."*
   c. *Don't sell steak -- sell sizzle.*

Lecturer's words

The US Patent Office has granted numerous patents for perpetual motion machines based upon applications with complete detailed drawings. Some years ago, though, the patent office began requiring working models of such a machine before a patent would be granted. Result: no patents granted for perpetual motion machines since that time.

Student's telegraphic sentence

Perpetual motion machine (drawings) = many patents.
Required working model = no patents since.

FIGURE 2.1 Examples of Telegraphic Sentences

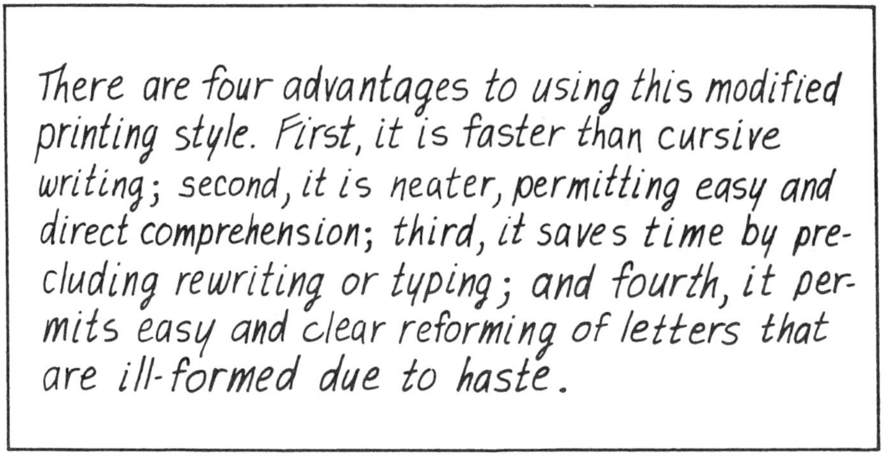

There are four advantages to using this modified printing style. First, it is faster than cursive writing; second, it is neater, permitting easy and direct comprehension; third, it saves time by precluding rewriting or typing; and fourth, it permits easy and clear reforming of letters that are ill-formed due to haste.

FIGURE 2.2   Modified Printing Style

The Two-Page System

When you need to scramble to keep up with a fast-talking lecturer, you may find this two-page system helpful. Here's the way it works: Lay your binder flat on the desk. On the left-hand page, record main ideas only. The left-hand page is your primary page. On the right-hand page, record as many details as you have time for. Place the details opposite the main ideas that they support. After the lecture, remain in your seat for a few minutes and fill in any gaps in your notes while the lecture is still relatively fresh in mind.

The Cassette and Tape Taboo

Do not use a tape or cassette recorder. If you do, you'll be wasting time and not learning very much. When a lecture is on tape, you cannot review it in five or ten minutes; you have to replay the entire lecture. Worst of all, you cannot use the technique of reciting, which is the most effective learning technique known to psychologists. Furthermore, you also lose the advantage of visual learning—that is, seeing the words and seeing the relationship between the written ideas.

Some students create written notes as they listen to the tape in the privacy of their rooms. Don't you see the waste of time? The notes could have been taken directly during the "live" lecture.

No Shorthand

Don't take lecture notes in shorthand. Shorthand notes cannot be studied effectively while they are still in symbol form. Besides, shorthand symbols still have to be transformed into regular words. If you need a fast method to keep up with the lecturer, use the abbreviations and the symbols listed at the end of this chapter.

No Typing

Scribbling is a bad habit. Write legibly the first time. Don't rationalize that you'll type your notes when you return to your room. Typing your notes is a waste of time, opportunity, and energy. You'll need almost a full hour to decipher and type one set of scribbled lecture notes. The hour you spend typing could have been extremely productive if you had spent it reciting notes taken during the lecture. Typing can exhaust you physically, mentally, and emotionally, leaving you unfit for the task of learning.

Contrary to what most people think, almost no learning takes place during the typing of scribbled notes. The act of deciphering and typing requires almost total concentration, leaving scant concentration for comprehending the facts and ideas being typed.

Signal Words and Phrases

Most college lecturers speak about 120 words per minute. In a fifty-minute lecture, you hear up to six thousand words expressing ideas, facts, and details. To impose some recognizable order on those ideas, facts, and details, lecturers use signal words and phrases.

Signal words and phrases themselves do not express ideas, facts, and details. They do, however, convey important information of a directional and relational sort. If you, as a note taker, know the importance and meaning of signal words and phrases, you'll be able to perceive the organization of the lecture, the direction of the lecture, and the relationship among the ideas, facts, and details. A list of signal words and phrases is given in Figure 2.3. Being able to recognize signal words and phrases will improve your reading, writing, speaking, and listening, as well as your note taking.

The Final Barrage

Pay close attention to the end of the lecture. Speakers who do not pace themselves well may have to cram half of the lecture into the last five or ten minutes. Record such packed finales as rapidly as you can. After class, stay in

Categories and Examples	When you hear these words, immediately think . . .

Example Words
    to illustrate
    for example
    for instance
	"Here comes an example. The lecturer wants to make clear the point just made. I'd better write this down; otherwise I'll forget it."

Time Words
    before, after
    formerly
    subsequently
    prior
    meanwhile
	"Hm-m! A time relationship is being established. Let's see, what came first and what came last, and what came in-between?"

Addition Words
    furthermore
    in addition
    moreover
    also
	"After listing everything, they always seem to have one more thing to add. Well, I'd better get it and write it down."

Cause and Effect Words
    therefore
    as a result
    if . . . then
    accordingly
    thus, so
	"There's that cause and effect word. I'd better quickly write down the word *effect* in my notes at this point. Later, I'll go back and write the word *cause* to label the preceding points."

Contrast Words
    on the other hand
    in contrast
    conversely
    pros and cons
	"Now we're getting the other side of the picture, the other person's story, the research that contradicts what has already been said."

Enumeration Words
    the four steps . . .
    first, second, third
    next
    finally
	"Ten steps is a lot! I'd better number them and list them in order."

Emphasis Words
    more importantly
    above all
    remember this
	"Sounds like a hint that this idea is something important and something to remember."

Repeat Words
    in other words
    in the vernacular
    it simply means
    that is, briefly
    in essence
	"Simplifying a complex idea or simplifying a long-winded explanation. I'd better note this simplified version."

FIGURE 2.3 Signal Words and Phrases

Categories and Examples	When you hear these words, immediately think . . .
Swivel Words however nevertheless yet, but still	"A warning that there's a little bit of doubt or 'give-back' on the point just made. I'd better note this qualifying remark."
Concession Words to be sure of course granted indeed though	"I see. These are similar to the swivel words. The lecturer is admitting that the opposition has a point or two."
Summary Words in a nutshell to sum up in conclusion	"Great! I'll try to get this summary word for word; then I can study it thoroughly when I get to my room."
Test Clues This is important. Remember this. You'll see this again. Here's a pitfall.	"Sounds like a potential test item. I'd better get this one word for word."

FIGURE 2.3   Signal Words and Phrases (*continued*)

your seat for a few extra minutes to write down as much as you can remember.

Instant Replay

As soon as you leave the lecture room, while walking to your next class, mentally recall the lecture from beginning to end. Visualize the classroom and the lecturer and any blackboard work. After mentally recalling the lecture, ask yourself some questions: What was the lecturer getting at? What really was the central point? What did I learn? How does what I learned fit in with what I already know? If you discover anything you don't quite understand, no matter how small, make a note of it and ask the instructor before the next class to explain it.

Avoiding Ice-Cold Notes

During your first free period after class, or that evening at the latest, read over your notes to fill in gaps and to give yourself an overview of the lecture.

Review your notes while the lecture is still fresh in your mind. Ice-cold notes are frustrating and are time wasters. Days after a lecture, you do not want to be gazing at your own writing and wondering, "What did I mean by that?"

Two Dozen Dos and One Dozen Don'ts

The twenty-four dos and twelve don'ts that follow are the warp and woof of note taking. Weave them into a magic carpet of your own design and glide over all the rough spots of note taking.

Dos

1. Look over previous notes before class. (Maintains continuity.)
2. Attend *all* lectures. (It's a continuing story.)
3. Be academically aggressive. (Sit up straight with "rolled-up sleeves.")
4. Take a front seat to see and hear better. (You won't dare snooze.)
5. Use a large, loose-leaf binder. (Gives ample room.)
6. Carry lined loose-leaf (8½ × 11) sheets to class. (Insert into binder on return.)
7. Write on only one side of sheet. (Spread out for review.)
8. On top sheet, record course, lecturer, and date. (In case of spill.)
9. Begin taking notes immediately. (Don't wait for inspiration.)
10. Write in short, telegraphic sentences. (Parsimoniously meaningful.)
11. Make notes complete for later understanding. (Don't sit there puzzling.)
12. Use modified printing style. (Clear letters, not scribbles.)
13. Use lecturer's words. (Lecturers like to see their words in exams.)
14. Strive to detect main headings. (As if you peeked at the lecturer's notes.)
15. Capture ideas as well as facts. (Get the drift too.)
16. Keep your note-organization simple. (Easy does it.)
17. Skip lines; leave space between main ideas. (Package the ideas.)
18. Discover the organizational pattern. (Like putting together a puzzle.)
19. If the lecture is too fast, capture fragments. (Jigsaw them together later.)
20. Leave blank spaces for words to fill in later. (Thus avoid voids.)
21. Develop your own abbreviations and symbols. (Not too many, but enough.)
22. Record lecturer's examples. (If you don't, you'll forget.)

23. Identify your own thought-notes. (What's mine? What's the lecturer's?)

24. Keep separate loose-leaf binders for each course. (Don't combine notes yet.)

Don'ts

1. Don't sit near friends. (Can be distracting.)

2. Don't wait for something "important." (Record everything.)

3. Don't convert lecturer's words. (Takes time and invites imprecision.)

4. Don't look for facts only. (See ideas too.)

5. Don't give up if the lecturer is too fast. (Some is better than none.)

6. Don't stop to ponder. (Do so later in your room.)

7. Don't over-indent. (You'll run out of right-side space.)

8. Don't doodle. (Breaks concentration and eye contact.)

9. Don't use spiral-bound notebooks. (Can't insert handouts.)

10. Don't consider any example too obvious. (Copy it!)

11. Avoid using Roman numerals. (You'll get tangled up.)

12. Avoid too many abbreviations. (Trouble deciphering later.)

THE CORNELL NOTE-TAKING SYSTEM

The notes you take in class are really a hand-written textbook. In many instances, your lecture notes are more practical, meaningful, and up-to-date than a textbook. If you keep them neat, complete, and well organized, they'll serve you splendidly.

To help students organize their notes, I developed the Cornell Note-taking System forty years ago at Cornell University. It is used in colleges not only in the United States but also in foreign countries, including China. The keystone of the system is a two-column note sheet.

Use 8½ by 11 paper to create the note sheet (see Figure 2.4). Down the left side, draw a vertical line 2½ inches from the edge of the paper. End this line 2 inches above the bottom of the paper. Draw a horizontal line across the bottom of the paper, 2 inches above the paper's edge. In the narrow (2½") column on the left, you will write cue words or questions. In the wide (6") column on the right, you will write lecture notes. In the space at the bottom of the sheet, you will summarize your notes. Note: You can use this system if you use lined notebook paper, too. You can disregard the red vertical rule and make your own rule 2½" from the left edge of the paper. Or you can make

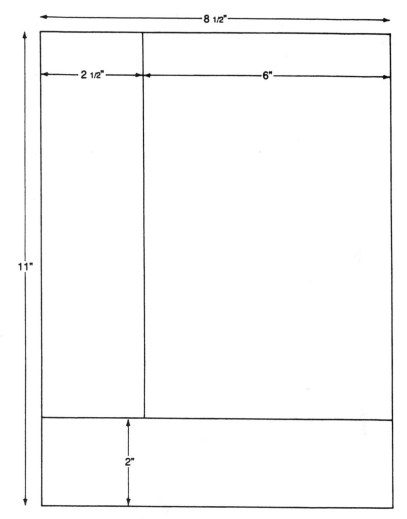

FIGURE 2.4 Note-Sheet Format for the Cornell Note-taking System
During a lecture class, the student writes notes in the wide (6″) column. To study from the notes, the student writes either cue words or questions in the narrow column and a summary in the space at the bottom of the note sheet.

the rule 2½" from the red rule, leaving yourself 4" for the wide note-taking column. In either case, you will have the 2½" left-hand space for important cue words and questions.

There are two versions of the Cornell System: (1) the Six R version, (2) the One Q/Five R version. Both versions have six steps. The main difference between them is in step 2. The six steps are listed in Table 2.1 and discussed in detail below. Notice that step 2 in the Six R version is *reduce*; in the One Q/Five R version, step 2 is *question*.

When you use the Six R version, you will write cue words in the narrow column of the note sheet (see Figure 2.5). When you use the One Q/Five R version, you will write questions in the narrow column (see Figure 2.6). Which version is better? Give each one a try, and see which one works best for you.

Step 1: Record

In the wide column, record as many facts and ideas as you can. Use telegraphic sentences, but make sure that weeks after the lecture your notes will still make sense. Write legibly. Directly after class or at your first opportunity, fill in any blank spaces that you left and clarify your handwriting if necessary.

Step 2: Reduce (<u>Six R version only</u>)

During your first study opportunity, reread your notes and rethink the entire lecture. Then reduce each fact and idea in your notes to key words and phrases. In the narrow column of the note sheet, jot down the word or phrase that you have extracted from the fact or idea. The key words and phrases will act as memory cues. Later, when you see or hear them, you will recall the full fact or idea.

TABLE 2.1   Steps in the Cornell Note-taking System

Step	Six R Version	One Q/Five R Version
1[a]	Record	Record
2	Reduce	Question
3	Recite	Recite
4	Reflect	Reflect
5	Review	Review
6[a]	Recapitulate	Recapitulate

[a]Notes made in class (step 1) and the summary written during study time (step 6) are placed in the wide column of the note sheet.

	Psych. 102 – Prof. Goldsmith – Sept. 14th (Mon.)
	A. Build Self-Confidence – 15 steps
Weaknesses & strengths	1. Assess strengths & weaknesses
	a. Set goals accordingly
Life's goal	2. Decide what you'd like your life to be
	a. Rework your thinking to bring inner script up to date
Negatives	3. Bury all _negative_ memories
	a. Forgive others & self
	b. Remember past successes - even minor ones
Guilt & shame	4. Wipe out any guilt & shame
	a. Don't allow these thoughts mental entrance
Personality defects	5. Don't attribute present behavior to personality defects
	a. Real causes might be economic, political, social, etc.
Points of view	6. Events may be seen differently by different people
	a. Rejections or put-downs might not be actual
Negative labels	7. Never label yourself negatively
	a. Such as: stupid, ugly, failure, incorrigible
Criticism	8. Accept criticism of a _specific_ action, but not of _you_ as a person
	a. Accept constructive criticism graciously
Failures blessing	9. Failures can be a blessing -- goals not right for you
	a. Avoids later let-down
Inadequacy	10. Don't tolerate people, jobs, situations that make you feel inadequate
	a. If can't change them or you -- walk out
Relax	11. Take time to relax & meditate -- hobbies
	a. Keep in touch w/ your inner self
Social	12. Be social -- enjoy other people
	a. See their needs and help them
Playing it too cool	13. Don't overprotect your ego -- it's resilient
	a. Better to try & fail, than to clam up - numbing!

Goals:
  long-range
  short-range
	14. Develop long-ranged goals, also short-ranged ones
	a. Evaluate progress & whisper word of praise in your own ear

Not an object - active actor - _live_ your life	15. You're not a passive object -- you can make things happen a. You're a product of millions of years of evolution & made in God's image b. Don't worry about _how_ to live your life, lose yourself -- be absorbed in _living_ it

Through deep thinking, decide what you want to be. What to do with your life. Write out long-term & short-term goals. Eliminate totally & permanently _all_ _negative_ feelings & occurrences past, present, & future. Do things. Try things. Ego can take set-backs. Don't withdraw to solitary "safety." Enter the stream of life. Be busy swimming in it.

FIGURE 2.5 The Six R Version
The narrow column contains key words and phrases.

Psych. 105 – Prof. Martin – Sept. 14 (Mon.)

MEMORY

A. Memory tricky – Can recall instantly many trivial things of childhood; yet, forget things recently worked hard to learn & retain.

B. Memory Trace

How do psychologists account for remembering?

1. Fact that we retain information means that some change was made in the brain.
2. Change called "memory trace."

What's a "memory trace"?

3. "Trace" probably a molecular arrangement similar to molecular changes in a magnetic recording tape.

C. Three memory systems: sensory, short-term, long-term.

What are the three memory systems?

1. Sensory (lasts one second)

How long does sensory memory retain information?

Ex. Words or numbers sent to brain by sight (visual image) start to disintegrate within a few tenths of a second & gone in one full second, unless quickly trans-

How is information transferred to STM?

ferred to S-T memory by verbal repetition.

2. Short-term memory [STM] (lasts 30 seconds)

What are the retention times of STM?

a. Experiments show: a syllable of 3 letters remembered 50% of the time after 3 seconds. Totally forgotten end of 30 seconds.

What's the capacity of the STM?

b. S-T memory-limited capacity=holds average of 7 items.
c. More than 7 items--jettisons some to make room.

How to hold information in STM?

d. To hold items in STM, must rehearse-- must hear sound of words internally or externally.

3. Long-Term memory [LTM] (lasts a lifetime or short time).

What are the retention times of LTM?

a. Transfer fact or idea by:
(1) Associating w/information already in LTM

What are the six ways to transfer information from STM to LTM?

(2) Organizing information into meaningful units
(3) Understanding by comparing & making relationships.
(4) Frameworking - fit pieces in like in a jigsaw puzzle.
(5) Reorganizing - combing new & old into a new unit.
(6) Rehearsing - aloud to keep memory trace strong

Three kinds of memory systems are sensory, which retains information for about one second; short-term, which retains for a maximum of thirty seconds; and long-term, which varies from a lifetime of retention to a relatively short time.

The six ways (activities) to transfer information to the long-term memory are: associating, organizing, understanding, frameworking, reorganizing and rehearsing.

FIGURE 2.6   The One Q/Five R Version
The narrow column contains questions.

Step 2: Question (<u>One Q/Five R version only</u>) _____

During your first opportunity, reread your notes and rethink the entire lecture. Then formulate questions based on your notes. In the narrow column of the note sheet, opposite the fact or idea in your notes, write a brief question that can be answered with the information in your notes. Writing questions helps to clarify meanings, reveal relationships, establish continuity, and strengthen memory. It also sets the stage for studying for exams.

Step 3: Recite _____

Reciting is saying each fact or idea in your notes out loud, in your own words, and from memory. Recitation is an extremely powerful aid to memory. Recitation makes you think, and thinking leaves a trace in your memory. Experiments show that students who recite retain 80 percent of the material; students who reread but do not recite retain only 20 percent when tested two weeks later. Without retention, there is no learning.

Cover up the wide column of your note sheet with a piece of blank paper, exposing only the cue words or questions in the narrow column. Read each cue word or question aloud; then recite *aloud* and in *your own words* the full facts and ideas brought to mind by the cue word or the answer to the question. After reciting, slide the blank sheet down to check your answer. If your answer is incomplete or incorrect, straighten out the information in your mind and then recite your answer aloud again. Recite until you get the answer right. Proceed through the entire lecture in this way.

Why recite aloud? The sound of your voice stimulates your thinking process. It is this thinking that leaves behind in your memory some neural trace to which you may return later, as to a filing cabinet, to retrieve a fact or idea. Reciting aloud is the most powerful single technique known to psychologists for implanting facts and ideas in your memory.

Why recite using your own words? Cognitive theorists have discovered that people do not remember verbatim what they hear or read. Rather, they remember the meaning that they gave to a fact or idea that they heard or read, and the meaning was expressed in words that they used when they were thinking about the fact or idea. In sum, you remember the meaning you gave to a fact or idea as you processed it in your mind through the use of your own words.

Step 4: Reflect _____

Professor Hans Bethe, nuclear physicist and Nobel Prize winner, said that "creativity comes only through reflection." Reflection is thinking about and applying the facts and ideas that you've learned. You reflect by asking yourself questions such as these: What is the significance of these facts? What principles are they based on? How can I apply them? How do they fit in with what I already know? What is beyond these facts and principles?

Reflection leads to advantageous learning—learning that is done voluntarily and with enthusiasm and curiosity, learning that is propelled by a burning desire to know something. What distinguishes advantageous learning from regular learning is your mental attitude. Knowledge gained through advantageous learning will still be with you long after you have taken your final examination.

Step 5: Review

As many students are aware, yesterday's knowledge interferes with today's knowledge and today's knowledge interferes with yesterday's knowledge. The battle between remembering and forgetting goes on continuously. The best way to prepare for examinations is to keep reviewing and keep reciting the sets of notes that you'll be held responsible for.

Every evening, before you settle down to study, quickly review your notes. Pick up a designated set of notes and recite them. Short, fast, frequent reviews will produce far better understanding and far better remembering than long, all-day or all-night sessions can. After reciting, move immediately into your regular study routine.

Step 6: Recapitulate

Writing a recapitulation, or summary, is not easy, but the rewards are great. Recapitulating is a sure-fire way to gain a deep understanding of the facts and ideas in your notes, and reviewing summaries makes studying for exams a breeze. If you take the time to summarize your notes, your understanding deepens because you have the whole picture instead of an assortment of facts.

Write your summary in the space below the horizontal line at the bottom of the note sheet. Summarize according to one of these plans:

1. Summarize the content of each note sheet.
2. Summarize the content of the entire lecture on the last note sheet for that lecture.
3. Do both 1 and 2.

The third option yields the greatest reward. When you review your notes for exams, you'll be able to see the steps you took to arrive at your final, last-page summary.

TYPES OF NOTES

There are various types of notes that you can use: topic-explanation notes, sentence notes, topic-idea notes, paragraph notes. The nature of the subject, the lecturer's style, and your personal preference will determine which you choose. Be sure to use the Cornell System format with all four types.

Topic-Explanation Notes

Take a look at Figure 2.7. When the lecturer said, "There are two kinds of magic used in many primitive societies," the note taker was ready to list and enumerate them. Notice that the note taker fortified the two kinds of magic with good examples. Later, the note taker wrote key words and phrases in the narrow column.

Sentence Notes

In most instances, sentence notes written in a telegraphic style will be the most efficient way to record a lecture. Be flexible, though, because (as Figure 2.8 shows) you might have to switch from one type of notes to another.

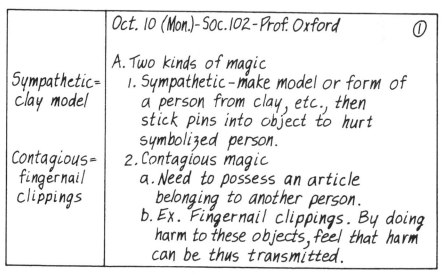

FIGURE 2.7 Topic-Explanation Notes

	Oct. 10 (Mon.) - Soc. 102 - Prof. Oxford ②

Stick has power
Power = mana
	A. Animism
	1. Object has supernatural power
	2. Power called <u>mana</u> (not limited to objects)
	  a. Objects accumulate mana
	    Ex. Good canoe - more mana than poor one.
	  b. Objects can lose mana

Can gain or
lose mana
	c. People collect objects w/lots of mana
	  d. Good person's objects collect mana
	  e. People, animals, plants have mana, too.

Good people have
lots of mana
	Ex. Expert canoe builder has mana —
	      imparts mana to canoe
	  f. Chief has lots of mana — dangerous to
	    get too close to chief—mana around head.

FIGURE 2.8 Sentence Notes

	Oct. 27 (WED.) - Economics 105 - Prof. Terry ①
	<u>Some Basic Laws & Principles</u>

What is the Law
of Diminishing
Returns?
	1. Law of Diminishing Returns
	  a. Refers to amount of extra output (pro-
	    duction) we get when we add additional
	    inputs; but, after a point, the extra inputs
	    yield decreasing amounts of extra output.

What is
Malthus's Law?
	b. Malthus's views depended on this law =
	    Just so much land, but population
	    could increase more rapidly than food
	    supplies.

FIGURE 2.9 Topic-Idea Notes

What is the Greek concept of a well-rounded man?	*Nov. 6 (MON) – World Lit. 106 – Prof Warnek* ①
	
	 <u>Greek Race</u>
	 1. Unity = well-rounded
	    Early Greeks vigorous. Goal was to be
	    well-rounded : unity of knowledge &
	    activity. No separate specializations as
	    law, literature, philosophy, etc. Believed
	    one man should master all things
	    equally well; not only knowledge, but be
	    an athlete, soldier, & statesman, too.

FIGURE 2.10   Paragraph Notes

Topic-Idea Notes

The topic-idea format is often useful in history, economics, and philosophy courses. The lecturer mentions a topic and then expands on it. Notice that in Figure 2.9 the "paragraph" about the law of diminishing returns is broken up by two subtopic indicators to show separate ideas.

Paragraph Notes

If the lecturer is expounding on an idea in a straightforward fashion, don't try to impose some sort of topic and subtopic organization where there is none. Instead, write short, telegraphic sentences and end up with an almost solid paragraph, as shown in Figure 2.10.

COMBINING TEXTBOOK AND LECTURE NOTES

The format shown in Figure 2.11 is ideal for lectures that mainly explain and amplify the textbook. First, in the middle column, record your notes on a previously assigned textbook chapter. Then, when you take lecture notes in the right-hand column, you can avoid repeating material you already have,

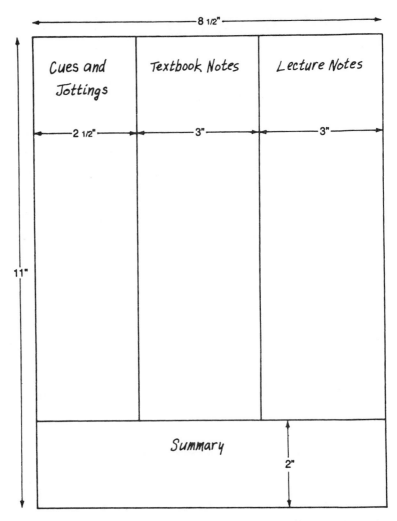

FIGURE 2.11   Cornell System Format for Combining Textbook and Lecture Notes

while you add the lecturer's explanations, examples, and supplementary comments. When you become accustomed to the lecturer's ways, you will be able to judge how much space to leave between items in the middle column in order to keep lecture notes and textbook notes directly opposite each other. The cue words or questions that you write in the left column should pull the two sets of notes together.

ABBREVIATIONS AND SYMBOLS

You should use only the abbreviations that fit your needs and that you will remember easily. A good idea is to introduce only a few abbreviations into your note taking at a time. Overuse may leave you with notes that are difficult to read. Here are some rules to keep in mind.

1. Symbols are especially helpful to students in engineering and mathematics. Lists of commonly used symbols are given in most textbooks and reference books.

$\neq$	does not equal
f	frequency

2. Create a family of symbols.

◯	organism
☉	individual
Ⓢ	individuals

3. Leave out the periods in standard abbreviations.

cf	compare
eg	for example
dept	department
NYC	New York City

4. Use only the first syllable of a word.

pol	politics
dem	democracy
lib	liberal
cap	capitalism

5. Use the entire first syllable and only the first letter of a second syllable.

subj	subject
cons	conservative
tot	totalitarianism
ind	individual

6. Eliminate final letters. Use just enough of the beginning of a word to form an easily recognizable abbreviation.

assoc	associate, associated
ach	achievement
biol	biological
info	information
intro	introduction
chem	chemistry
conc	concentration
max	maximum
rep	repetition

7. Omit vowels from the middle of words, and retain only enough consonants to provide a recognizable skeleton of the word.

bkgd	background
ppd	prepared
prblm	problem
estmt	estimate
gvt	government

8. Use an apostrophe.

gov't	government
am't	amount
cont'd	continued
educat'l	educational

9. Form the plural of a symbol or abbreviated word by adding "s."

☐s	areas
chaps	chapters
co-ops	cooperatives
f̲s	frequencies
/s	ratios

10. Use "g" to represent *ing* endings.

decrg	decreasing
ckg	checking
estg	establishing
exptg	experimenting

11. Use a dot placed over a symbol or word to indicate the word *rate*.

$\dot{\updownarrow}$	vibration rate
$\dot{f}$	frequency rate

12. Generally, spell out short words such as *in, at, to, but, for,* and *key*. Symbols, signs, or abbreviations for short words will make the notes too dense with "shorthand."

13. Leave out unimportant verbs.

14. Leave out the words *a* and *the*.

15. If a term, phrase, or name is initially written out in full during the lecture, substitute initials whenever the term, phrase, or name is used again.
Initial writing: Modern Massachusetts Party
Subsequently: MMP

16. Use symbols for commonly recurring connective or transitional words.

&	and
w/	with
w/o	without
vs	against
∴	therefore

SUMMARY

Why should I take notes?	The answer is simple: because forgetting is massive and instantaneous. Forgetting wipes out information like a tornado. Note taking provides disaster relief.
What do the research of Hermann Ebbinghaus and the Leon-Clyde anecdote demonstrate?	Ebbinghaus found that in just twenty minutes we lose nearly half of what we've learned. The Leon-Clyde episode showed how quickly two intelligent men can forget the key points of a lecture that both thought was brilliant. Both point to the necessity of taking notes to combat forgetting.
How do I begin taking notes?	A good way to start is with telegraphic sentences. Students who try to write down a lecture word for word are asking for trouble. The secret is to record only the key words. This streamlined version will save you time, yet provide you with the information you need.
What's the best way to take notes—with printing or with cursive?	Neither. Use the modified printing style. It provides the best of both worlds. It's fast and neat, and it saves you time that you might otherwise spend recopying.
Are there some time wasters in note taking?	Yes. There are at least three that you should avoid: (1) Never tape a lecture. (2) Don't use shorthand. (3) Don't recopy or type your notes.
How can I use the speaker's signals to my advantage?	Expressions such as "in contrast to" or "to sum up" act as signals and help you identify the pattern of organization the speaker is following. If you can follow the speaker's organizational pattern, you'll have little trouble fitting in the facts and ideas along the way.
What do you mean by instant replay?	As soon as you've left the classroom, take a moment to relive the lecture mentally from start to finish. After you've replayed the lecture in your mind, take a few moments to reflect on what the instructor has said and what it all means.

When should I review my notes?	Right away if possible. The longer you wait, the more you'll forget. Review your notes while the lecture is still fresh in your mind.
What is the Cornell Note-taking System?	The Cornell System is a time-honored technique for getting the most out of your notes. The keystone of the system is its format, a 6-inch area for your lecture notes and a 2½-inch left-hand margin for cue words or questions. There are two versions of the Cornell System: the Six R version and the One Q/Five R version. Both have six steps. The main difference between them is in step 2.
What is step 1?	Step 1, recording, simply involves taking notes. The notes go in the 6-inch column. Record as many of the lecturer's key ideas as you can. Use telegraphic sentences to get the information on paper quickly.
What is step 2?	Step 2 in the Six R version is reducing the key facts in your notes to cue words. Step 2 in the One Q/Five R version is formulating some cue questions.
What are cue words?	Cue words are key words or phrases written in the 2½-inch column that act as cues to help you to recall a full fact or idea.
How do I use cue questions?	Simply dream up a question that can be answered with the information from a full fact or idea.
What is involved in step 3, reciting?	When you recite, you say each key fact or idea in your notes out loud, in your own words, and from memory. If you are using the Six R version, your memory will be triggered by the key words in the 2½-inch margin. If you are using the One Q/Five R version, a thoughtful question will focus your response. In either case, the fact that you recite out loud will reveal immediately whether your answer is correct.
What is the reflection step?	Reflection involves thinking about and applying the concepts and ideas that you

learn. It triggers advantageous learning—learning that is done voluntarily and with enthusiasm. Advantageous learning has the best chance of lasting.

How often should I follow step 5, reviewing?

As often as possible. Reviewing is really the workhorse of both methods. How much you review will determine whether you will be able to remember important information days and weeks from now. If you make an effort to do a quick review of your notes every evening before you begin studying, you'll do a good job of maintaining your hard-earned knowledge.

What about the sixth and final step, recapitulation?

In short, it means summarizing. If you take the time to summarize your notes, your understanding will deepen because you'll have the whole picture.

Is there more than one way to summarize?

Yes. You have three choices: (1) Summarize the content of each note sheet. (2) Summarize the entire lecture at the bottom of the last note sheet for that lecture. (3) Do both 1 and 2. The third choice is worth the extra effort.

Can lecture and textbook notes be combined?

Yes. Combining lecture and textbook notes is especially important if the lecturer repeats what is in the textbook. Use a three-column format: one column for your lecture notes, another for the notes from your textbook, and the third for your cue words or questions.

Are abbreviations and symbols a help in note taking?

Used sparingly, abbreviations and symbols can be a help. A few key abbreviations can save you time and space. If you use too many abbreviations and symbols, your notes will be difficult to read.

HAVE YOU MISSED SOMETHING?

1. *Sentence completion.* Complete the following sentences with one of the three words listed below each sentence.

   a. Much of the information that a person receives is no longer available after a few _____.

   minutes   hours   weeks

   b. The Leon-Clyde anecdote illustrates the problem of _____.

   note taking   forgetting   recapitulation

2. *Matching.* In each blank space in the left column, write the number preceding the phrase in the right column that matches the left item best.

_____ a. Two-page system	1. Can reveal where the lecture is heading
_____ b. Forgetting	2. Used cue words or questions
_____ c. Cornell System	3. Is both instant and massive
_____ d. 2½-inch column	4. Ideal format for coping with speedy lecturers
_____ e. 6-inch column	5. Is not recommended as a method of note taking
_____ f. Recapitulation	6. Used for classroom lecture notes
_____ g. Shorthand	7. Time-tested method for taking notes
_____ h. Signal words	8. Note-taking step that involves writing summaries

3. *True-false.* Write *T* beside the *true* statements and *F* beside the *false* statements.

   _____ a. Notes written in the modified printing style must be retyped.

   _____ b. Nearly 47 percent of material learned is forgotten in just twenty minutes.

   _____ c. Taping the lecture is an efficient way to get all the information you need.

   _____ d. Almost no learning takes place during the act of typing.

   _____ e. A well-written stack of notes can function as a second textbook.

   _____ f. The last five or ten minutes of a lecture often contain the greatest concentration of information.

4. *Note-taking dos.* Write "yes" next to the tips that are recommended for optimal note taking.

   _____ a. Look over your previous notes before class.

   _____ b. Use Roman numerals in outlining your notes.

   _____ c. Capture the ideas as well as the facts.

   _____ d. Differentiate your thoughts from the lecturer's thoughts.

   _____ e. Write on both sides of your note sheets.

   _____ f. Skip lines and leave space between main ideas.

   _____ g. Begin taking notes immediately.

   _____ h. Keep your notes in spiral-bound books.

5. *Multiple choice.* Choose the phrase that completes the following sentence most accurately, and circle the letter that precedes it.

   Telegraphic sentences provide you with

   a. verbatim notes
   b. a secretary-style transcription
   c. streamlined information
   d. typed documentation

CHAPTER 3

Learning from Your Textbooks

There is a great difference between knowing a thing and understanding it.

Charles Kettering (1876–1958), American electrical engineer and inventor

Are you going hungry? Some students devour their textbook assignments, yet never learn a thing. That's because learning from a textbook involves more than just reading. It means digesting what you read. A textbook assignment needs to be read actively in order to provide food for thought. This chapter discusses

- Getting acquainted with your textbooks
- Mining prefaces and introductions
- Study systems for textbooks

specifically

- The SQ3R Method
- 3Rs for academic survival

and finally

- The Questions-in-the-Margin System

**B**ecause you and your textbooks are going to spend a quarter or a semester together, you'd better become friends. How? By getting acquainted.

GETTING ACQUAINTED WITH YOUR TEXTBOOKS

Buy all your textbooks immediately after you register. This is a wise policy even if your school allows a period in which you can attend many courses before deciding on a final few. Get a head start by reading the tables of contents, prefaces, introductions, and any other up-front material in all your books. Underline important words and sentences, and make notes in the margins. (Of course, if you think you may not ultimately take a course whose books you've bought, don't make these marks! Save your receipts to return all unused books.) Then, while you still have the time, leaf through each of your books. Look at the pictures, tables, and diagrams; read the captions. Read chapter titles and headings and subheadings that interest you. This will give you a good idea of what the book is like and where you will be going during the semester. Later, you'll be glad you did, for you'll be able to see how the various parts of the course fit together.

Reading the Preface _____

The authors of most textbooks are dealing with serious subjects. Consequently, they write in a serious, scholarly vein. They may be warm and congenial people, but they can appear, in their writing, to be cold and faceless. The only place where most authors can drop their scholarly style and let their hair down is in the preface. There you have a chance to meet and get to know the authors as people. Once you do, you'll find that you can converse and even argue with them as you read the text. Now and then, you'll find yourself saying, "No, I don't agree with that statement" or "What do you mean by that?" You wouldn't make such a statement to a cold, unanswering textbook if you couldn't visualize a live hand behind the writing.

Every textbook would be much more meaningful if the authors could visit your classroom and give a short, informal talk. Thereafter, your textbooks would have far greater meaning. Since personal appearances are usually out of the question, the next best thing is to let the authors talk with you in the preface.

For instance, one student struck pay dirt on page 54 of a ninety-page preface to *A Treatise of Human Nature* by David Hume (1711–76), a Scottish philosopher. Hume wrote in his preface, "If I find the root of human nature, I'll be able to explain all human actions." The student accurately interpreted this sentence to mean that Hume would be using a psychological and not a traditional philosophical approach. Thus, with this proper mental set established, the student was able to read Hume's *Treatise* fairly rapidly and with clear understanding. Students who had not read the author's long preface read the book with a mental set directed at ascertaining Hume's philosophy. Most of those students never understood what David Hume was trying to explain.

In prefaces you can find valuable information such as (1) what the author's objective is, (2) what the author's objective is not, (3) the organizational plan of the book, (4) how and why the book is different from other books about the same subject, and (5) the author's qualifications for writing the book. As a practical exercise, you might find it interesting to read the preface of this book, if you have not already done so. See how much you can gain toward understanding not only the book but also the author.

What the Author's Perspective Is and Is Not

This little book aims to give a certain perspective on the subject of language rather than to assemble facts about it. It has little to say of the ultimate psychological basis of speech and gives only enough of the actual descriptive or historical facts of particular languages to illustrate principles.[1]

It is a tremendous advantage to know the author's objective, for then you'll read and interpret the text from the correct point of view. Otherwise, reading could be quite a struggle, and the facts could seem to be completely unconnected. The author of the quotation just given is saying, "Keep your eye on the *perspective,* not on the facts." Being told what the author is *not* trying to do helps make the objective even clearer. Here, the author says, in effect, "No, this is not a list of facts, as many other books are." Being so warned, you'll refrain from drifting into the wrong pathway of thought while you are reading.

The Organizational Plan of the Book

This book is organized, therefore, neither along chronological lines nor the less obvious logical line of proceeding from simple narration to varying emphases. The arrangement is, if anything, psychological.[2]

Having the organizational plan is like having a road map. You'll know not only what the authors are doing but also where they are going. In the

---

[1] Edward Sapir, *Language* (New York: Harcourt Brace Jovanovich, 1921), p. v.
[2] William M. Sale, Jr., James Hall, and Martin Steinmann, Jr., eds., *Short Stories: Tradition and Direction* (Norfolk, Conn.: New Directions, 1949), p. xii.

example above, you're told what patterns the editors of the anthology are following and not following, which makes the plan of the book especially clear.

How and Why the Book Is Different

Many histories of philosophy exist, and it has not been my purpose merely to add one to their number. My purpose is to exhibit philosophy as an integral part of social and political life; not as the isolated speculations of remarkable individuals.[3]

Knowing how and why the book is different is valuable information. It is easy to think that a new book on a subject is just "more of the same old stuff." When authors point out why their book is different and why their version or approach is necessary, you will read with greater awareness and greater comprehension.

The Author's Qualifications

It is obviously impossible to know as much about every philosopher as can be known about him by a man whose field is less wide; I have no doubt that every single philosopher whom I have mentioned, with the exception of Leibniz, is better known to many men than to me. If, however, this were considered a sufficient reason for respectful silence, it would follow that no man should undertake to treat of more than some narrow strip of history.[4]

Writers usually try, in some subtle way, to let the reader know that their book is written by a scholar, an expert on the subject. In the example above, the writer develops a very fine logical point in an interesting manner. He admits that he is an expert on the German philosopher Leibniz (1646–1716) but not on the broad field of philosophy. He maintains that his lack of knowledge will not prevent him from writing on the broad topic because if writers tackled only their pet subjects, no one would be able to give an overview on any subject.

Reading the Introduction _____

There are four good reasons to read the introduction to a book:

1. The introduction is usually well written, because the writer knows that it is the book's show window—especially for prospective customers looking the book over to decide whether to buy it.

---

[3]Bertrand Russell, *A History of Western Philosophy* (New York: Simon and Schuster, Inc., and London: George Allen Unwin, Ltd., 1945), p. x.
[4]Ibid.

2. Having only limited space, the writer packs the introduction with facts and ideas. As a reader, you will gain a lot from reading a relatively few pages.

3. Reading the introduction puts you on firm footing for the rest of the book, making future assignments easier, requiring less time, and helping you achieve a higher level of mastery than you otherwise would have achieved.

4. With your underlinings and notes in the margin, you can quickly review the introduction time after time, to give yourself a warm-up as well as a door into each assigned chapter.

Figure 3.1 is a densely packed introduction containing information of great and immediate value for the sharper reading of textbooks. It is from a book titled *Six-Way Paragraphs.*[5] The book's sole purpose is to teach students how to spot main ideas. One hundred paragraphs are provided for practice. To prepare students for such practice, the introduction strives to explain the ins and outs of the paragraphs found in textbooks. As you read it, be aware of not only *what* the writer says but also *how* he says it and his *purpose* for saying it.

STUDY SYSTEMS FOR TEXTBOOKS

The old saying "Practice makes perfect" holds true for most activities. Is it true for the reading of textbook chapters? Some say it is not. Others say it is if the reader uses a specially constructed system to read and study the textbook chapters.

In the remainder of this chapter, you will be reading about three specially constructed systems: (1) the SQ3R Method, an old standby; (2) the 3Rs System, which consists of just three essential steps; (3) the Questions-in-the-Margin Technique, which is brand new. If one of these systems fits your personality, style, and academic needs, then adopt it. If you can't find a perfect fit, then select, modify, and adjust the parts of these three systems. Tailor one so that it is right for you.

THE SQ3R METHOD

The SQ3R Method was devised during World War II by Francis P. Robinson, an Ohio State University psychologist. The aim of the system was to help military personnel enrolled in special programs at the university to read

---

[5]Walter Pauk, *Six-Way Paragraphs* (Providence, R.I.: Jamestown Publishers, 1974).

what: wants you to focus on the paragraph - unit

how: brings you and the writer together

purpose: wants you to look at the paragraph through the eyes of the writer

what: each paragraph has but one main idea

how: shows you how a writer thinks

purpose: to convince you to look for only one idea per paragraph because writers follow this rule

what: the topic of the main idea is in the topic sentence, which is usually the first one

how: the writer needs to state a topic sentence to keep his own writing clear and under control

purpose: to instill confidence in you that the topic sentence is an important tool in a writer's kit and convince you it is there, so, look for it!

what: developing main ideas through supporting material

how: "more to a writer's job," still keeps you in the writer's shoes

purpose: to announce and advance the new step of supporting materials

what: (a) main ideas are often supported by examples, (b) other supporting devices listed

how: still through the writer's eyes

The paragraph! That's the working-unit of both writer and reader. The writer works hard to put meaning into the paragraph; the reader works hard to take meaning out of it. Though they work at opposite tasks, the work of each is closely related. Actually, to understand better the job of the reader, one must first understand better the job of the writer. So, let us look briefly at the writer's job.

To make his meaning clear, a writer knows that he must follow certain basic principles. First, he knows that he must develop only one main idea per paragraph. This principle is so important that he knows it backwards, too. He knows that he must not try to develop two main ideas in the same, single paragraph.

The next important principle he knows is that the topic of each main idea must be stated in a topic sentence and that such a sentence best serves its function by coming at or near the beginning of its paragraph. He knows, too, that the more clearly he can state the topic of his paragraph in an opening sentence, the more effective he will be in developing a meaningful, well-organized paragraph.

Now, there is more to a writer's job than just writing paragraphs consisting of only bare topic sentences and main ideas. The balance of his job deals with *developing* each main idea through the use of supporting material which amplifies and clarifies the main idea and many times makes it more vivid and memorable.

To support his main ideas, a writer may use a variety of forms. One of the most common forms to support a main idea is the *example*. Examples help to illustrate the main idea more vividly. Other

purpose: to develop the new idea
    of supporting materials

supporting materials are anecdotes, inci-
dents, jokes, allusions, comparisons, con-
trasts, analogies, definitions, exceptions,
logic, and so forth.

what: paragraph contains (a).
    topic sentence, (b) main
    idea, and (c) supporting
    material

how: transfer the knowledge
    from the writer to you,
    the reader

purpose: to summarize all the
    three steps

To summarize, the reader should
have learned from the writer that a text-
book-type paragraph usually contains these
three elements: a topic sentence, a main
idea, and supporting material. Knowing
this, the reader should use the topic sentence to lead him to the main idea. Once
he grasps the main idea, then everything
else is supporting material used to illustrate, amplify, and qualify the main idea.
So, in the final analysis, the reader must
be able to separate the main idea from the
supporting material, yet see the relationship between them.

FIGURE 3.1 The Content of an Introduction
Source: From Six-Way Paragraphs by Walter Pauk. Copyright © 1974 by Jamestown
Publishers, Providence, Rhode Island. Reprinted by permission.

faster and to study better. The letters in the name of the system stand for
survey, question, read, recite, and *review.* Robinson described the SQ3R Method
and explained its benefits:

> These five steps of the SQ3R system—survey, question, read, recite, and
> review—should result in faster reading, and fixing of the important points in
> the memory. You will find one other worthwhile outcome: Quiz questions will
> seem familiar because the headings turned into questions are usually the points
> emphasized in quizzes. By predicting actual quiz questions and looking up the
> answers beforehand, you know that you are effectively studying what is
> considered important in the course.[6]

The five steps of the SQ3R Method are described and explained as
follows[7]:

---

[6]Francis P. Robinson, *Effective Study,* 4th ed. (New York: Harper & Row, 1970), p. 32.
[7]Explanation and adaptation of five steps of the "SQ3R Method" from *Effective Study* Fourth
Edition by Francis P. Robinson. Copyright 1941, 1946 by Harper & Row, Publishers, Inc.
Copyright © 1961, 1970 by Francis P. Robinson. Reprinted by permission of Harper & Row,
Publishers, Inc.

S Survey

Glance through all the headings in the chapter, and read the final summary paragraph (if the chapter has one). This survey should not take more than a minute, and it will show you the three to six core ideas on which the discussion will be based. This orientation will help you organize the ideas as you read them later.

Q Question

Now begin to work. Turn the first heading into a question. This will arouse your curiosity and thereby increase comprehension. It will bring to mind information you already know, thus helping you understand that section more quickly. The question also will make important points stand out from explanatory details. You can turn a heading into a question as you read the heading, but it demands conscious effort on your part.

R_1 Read

Read so as to answer that question, but read only to the end of the first section. This should not be a passive plodding along each line, but an active search for the answer.

R_2 Recite

Having read the first section, look away from the book and try briefly to recite the answer to your question. Use your own words, and cite an example. If you can do this, you know what is in the book; if you cannot, glance over the section again. An excellent way to do this reciting from memory is to jot down brief cue phrases in outline form on a sheet of paper.

Now repeat the second to fourth steps for each successive section: That is, turn the next heading into a question, read to answer that question, and recite the answer by jotting down cue phrases in your outline. Read in this way until the entire lesson is completed.

R_3 Review

When you have read through in this way, look over your notes to get a bird's-eye view of the points and their relationships to each other. Check your memory by reciting the major subpoints under each heading. This can be done by covering up your notes and trying to recall the main points. Then expose each major point and try to recall the subpoints listed under it.

3Rs FOR ACADEMIC SURVIVAL

The 3Rs System is perfect for students who like to move quickly into a textbook chapter, or for those who face exams with little time for intensive study. The three Rs stand for *read, record,* and *recite*—the three essential steps for mastering textbook assignments. If you like its simplicity, you can also use the 3Rs System to implant facts and ideas in your long-term memory. Just emphasize the third step: Keep reciting the facts and ideas until overlearning occurs.

R_1 Read

Read several paragraphs; then go back to the first paragraph and ask yourself, "What do I need to know in this paragraph?" Read and reread until you find out.

R_2 Record

Once you have identified and can briefly say aloud what you need to know, underline only the key words, phrases, and sentences that identify this information. Later, when you review, your eyes will immediately focus on these, the essential parts of the paragraph. You won't have to reread the whole paragraph again when you review. Then do one more important thing: Jot in the margin an ever-so-brief question that asks for the information underlined. Question forming is very important in this system. Go through the entire chapter paragraph by paragraph.

R_3 Recite

Start at the first page of your assignment and cover up the printed page with a blank sheet of paper, leaving the questions in the margin exposed. Then, in your own words, recite aloud the answers. After reciting, check for accuracy. Recite until you've completed the chapter. Remember: If you don't know the answer now, you won't know it tomorrow in class or be able to write it on an exam. So, while you still have the chance, keep trying until you get the answer right.

THE QUESTIONS-IN-THE-MARGIN SYSTEM

The Questions-in-the-Margin System incorporates seven important steps needed to master any subject. Each step thoroughly done in sequence will

SURVEY	Read the title and speculate about what the chapter will be about. Read the headings to determine what ideas and facts will be presented. Read any summarizing section.
QUESTION	Turn each heading into a question by adding such words as "what," "how," or "who." Then read to answer the question.
READ	Read several paragraphs; then come back to the first paragraph and ask questions such as these: What is the main idea? How do the supporting materials support it? What do I need to know in this paragraph?
QUESTIONS IN MARGINS	Think deeply; then formulate and write a brief, telegraphic question in the margin. Next, underline very sparingly only the key words and phrases that make up the answer. The less underlining, the better.
RECITE	Counteract forgetting by reciting. Cover your textbook page, exposing only your questions in the margin. Then, in your own words, recite aloud the answers. After reciting, check for accuracy. Recite until you've completed the chapter.
REVIEW	Immediately after reciting, take a fresh look at each question; mentally glimpse and hold the answer for a few moments. In this way, work through the entire chapter. This overview of questions and answers will tend to snap the separate parts together like pieces of a jigsaw puzzle, enabling you to see the chapter as a whole. Intersperse reviews throughout the semester.
REFLECT	Manipulate the ideas and facts mentally. Turn them over, speculate on them, compare one with the other, notice where they agree and differ. Organize them under larger categories, or compress them into smaller units. Finally, free them from the chapter by weaving them into your existing knowledge.

FIGURE 3.2   The Questions-in-the-Margin System

help you see the author's facts and ideas more and more clearly. When you finish the seventh step, you will feel as though you had put the last piece of a jigsaw puzzle in place: You will see the full picture, which will image itself indelibly in your memory. Figure 3.2 is an overview of the system.

Step 1: Surveying a Textbook Chapter

Surveying has various uses, but its greatest use is in mastering textbook assignments. It is the grease that makes subsequent reading and studying more efficient. A good scholar would no more begin reading a chapter without first skimming it than an automotive engineer would run a car without first greasing it. The grease does not supply the power, but without it the gasoline would not be of much use.

If you skip this step, you will lose time, not save time. If you burrow directly into one paragraph after another, you'll be unearthing one compartmentalized fact after another, but you won't see how the facts relate to each other. Psychologists call this not-seeing-the-big-picture condition *tunnel vision.*

Here is how a student who had developed the technique of surveying to a fine art described this step:

> I first spend two or three minutes trying to get the full meaning out of the title of the chapter. I even wonder briefly why the author picked such a title. Then I shove off by saying to myself, "Let's see what he has to say about this subject."
>
> Next, I read the first couple of paragraphs in the regular way. If I don't do this, it's like coming into the middle of a conversation: I can't make head or tail of it.
>
> Then I let the printer guide me. My eyes dart to the big-type headings and subheadings. I read them because I know that they are like the small headlines for newspaper items. They are little summaries. I then read a sentence or two underneath these headings. My eyes float over the rest of the material looking for other islands of information. They might be marked by clues such as italicized words, underlined words, and changes in the type.
>
> When I first started to skim, I used to skip all the illustrations, charts, and diagrams. But after getting burned on exams, I found I could learn a lot very easily just by reading the captions and noticing what the lines on the diagrams and graphs meant. At least for me, illustrations stick in my mind better than words do; so during an exam, I take advantage of this. I close my eyes and see the illustration on the blackboard of my mind.
>
> I'm always careful to read the last paragraph or last section marked "summary." That's where the author gathers together all the main ideas of the chapter.
>
> Finally, I pause for a few minutes to bring all these pieces and fragments together before I begin reading and taking notes on the chapter. Sometimes to bring things together, I go back to the beginning of the chapter and leaf through the pages without reading, just looking at what I have already looked at.
>
> There are a few other things that skimming does for me. First, I no longer put off studying. Skimming is easy, so I don't mind getting started. Second, once I get into the chapter, I find that most of the chapters contain some interesting information, so I become interested. Third, because I am interested in the material, I concentrate better. And fourth, the topics that I find by skimming somehow make good topic headings for my notes.

When you skim, don't dawdle. Move along with good comprehension, but go slowly enough to get the facts, ideas, and principles accurately. Once assimilated, a mistake is hard to eradicate.

There are four practical reasons why surveying can make a real and immediate difference in your reading.

1. Surveying Creates a Background.   When you don't have some prior knowledge about the subject matter of an assigned chapter, you read slowly and have difficulty understanding the material. When you come to something that you recognize, your reading speed quickens and your comprehension grows. The difference is your prior knowledge. Surveying prepares you for reading by giving you some background information about a chapter. Surveying counteracts tunnel vision. Once you have viewed the broad canvas, you will see how individual ideas fit into the complete picture.

When you skim a chapter, you spot and pick up topics by reading headings and subheadings. You pick up ideas by reading the first and last sentences of paragraphs. You become familiar with the names of people and places by skimming these names. You grasp the general objective of the chapter by reading the introductory paragraph, and you get an overview by reading the summarizing paragraph at the end of the chapter. You won't know any of these facts and ideas cold, of course. But when you meet them again during your careful reading, you will recognize them, and this familiarity will give you confidence and understanding.

2. Surveying Provides Advance Organizers.   According to David P. Ausubel, a learning-theory psychologist, a preview of the general content of a chapter creates *advance organizers,* which help students learn and remember material they later study closely. The familiar landmarks act as topics or categories under which ideas, facts, and details may be clustered. John Livingston Lowes, a professor of literature at Princeton University, characterized such familiar landmarks as *magnetic centers* around which ideas, facts, and details cluster like iron filings around a magnet.

George Katona, a psychologist, tested the effectiveness of advance organizers with two groups of students. One group was asked to read a selection in which a general principle of economics was stated in the first sentence. The second group was given the same selection, but with the first sentence deleted. When the students in the first group were tested, they not only remembered the specific content of the paragraph better than the second group, but they were able to apply the general principle to all the examples in the selection. Without the first sentence, which was an advance organizer, students in the second group viewed the examples as separate, unrelated entities and were unable to see that the examples could be clustered under the one umbrella of a common principle in economics.

3. Surveying Limbers the Mind.   For an athlete, a pregame warm-up limbers muscles, and it also limbers the psyche and brain. An athlete knows that success comes from the coordination of smoothly gliding muscles, a positive attitude, and a concentrating mind. The prestudy survey of a text-book achieves for the scholar what the pregame warm-up achieves for the athlete.

4. Surveying Overcomes Mental Inertia.   How often have you said with impatience and exasperation, "Let's get started!" Getting started is hard. According to Newton's first law of motion, "A body in motion tends to remain in motion; a body at rest tends to remain at rest."

Many students find it difficult to open a textbook and begin to study. If you are one of them, use surveying to ease yourself into studying. Surveying does the job: It gets you started.

You need not always survey an entire chapter as the first step. You may begin by surveying the first part before you read it. Later, as you work your way through the chapter, you may want to skim farther ahead, page by page, as you read and study to understand.

Step 2: Turning Headings into Questions

The people who have *answers to give* when they are finished reading are usually those who had *questions to ask* before and during their reading. Asking questions works for one main reason: The questions force you to concentrate and to observe the words keenly, directly, and selectively as you read. When you don't have a question in mind, your eyes just glide over a paragraph, and you never realize that the printed words are alive with answers. In the words of John Lubbock (1834–1913), naturalist, banker, writer, neighbor of Charles Darwin, and coiner of the words *paleolithic* and *neolithic,* "What we see depends mainly on what we look for."

As you read, you should interrogate the writer, not simply stare at the words. You must approach each paragraph like an inquiring reporter, with definite and searching questions. The better your questions, the better will be your comprehension.

How do you formulate warm-up questions as you read and study a text-book? One technique is to turn each heading into a question. For example, the main heading "Basic Aspects of Memory" could be turned into the question "What are the basic aspects of memory?" The technique is simple, but it works. Here are some additional examples:

Subtopic Heading	*Question Formulated*
The Memory Trace	What is a memory trace?
Rate of Forgetting	How fast do we forget?
Organization of Recall	How is recall organized?
Decay Theory	What is the decay theory?

Once you have turned a heading into a question, you read the material under the heading to answer your question. If the question is answered early in the discussion, ask another, based on what you have read.

There are general questions that you can use in reading about almost any topic. Some readers prefer to ask these general questions to uncover specific facts and ideas. Other readers just enjoy conversing with the writer through the use of a general question-and-answer technique. In either case, an active, searching attitude is created. Here are some of the general questions:

- What does this paragraph tell me?
- What are the important supporting details?
- Does this example make the main point clear?
- What evidence does the writer give?
- What is the underlying principle?
- If this fact or idea is true, then what logically follows?
- If it is true, how does it affect my existing knowledge?
- How does this paragraph fit in with this chapter?
- What questions might I be asked about this paragraph?

Some practical readers ask not only "What is the author saying?" but also "How can I use this information?" If you ask such questions, make it a rule to try to answer them. Say something. Say anything that makes sense to you. Without effort, there's no gain.

A great deal is said these days about learning how to think: Books are written; lectures are given; and teachers exhort. The subject of thinking can be summarized in this one line: Thinking at its highest level is asking the right, relevant question.

Step 3: Reading Paragraph by Paragraph

After surveying the chapter, return to the first paragraph and read it thoroughly enough to answer only one question: What did the author say in this paragraph? If you are unable to answer this question at first, you must reread the paragraph until you can; otherwise you will not gain a functional understanding of the paragraph.

This is a crucial step. You must not move ahead to succeeding paragraphs if doing so means leaving the present paragraph unsettled. You may push on beyond a problem paragraph for the purpose of gaining context, but always with the intention of coming back to the problem paragraph. Remember that understanding a succession of paragraphs leads to comprehension of the chapter.

Guard against the habit of moving your eyes over the lines of print without grasping the writer's ideas. Read for the ideas and concepts behind the words. Pause at the end of each paragraph or at the end of a series of paragraphs, and in your own words describe the writer's main idea and the supporting details. Answer the question "What did I learn in this paragraph?" When you have described, you have understood.

The Topic Sentence. Use the topic sentence to help you break into the meaning of each paragraph. The topic sentence often contains the main idea or points to the main idea.

In Figure 3.3, the first sentence, the topic sentence, states the main idea. The rest of the paragraph is a long list of concrete examples supporting the main idea. The last sentence is not a continuation of the list; it rounds out or completes the paragraph. Incidentally (but importantly), notice how the writer sustains the mood of despondency from the opening sentence, through the examples, into the last clause of the last sentence.

Textbook Troubleshooting. As you read and study your textbook, your businesslike side should keep asking, "Am I getting it?" If the answer is, "It's getting pretty vague," you should take immediate action.

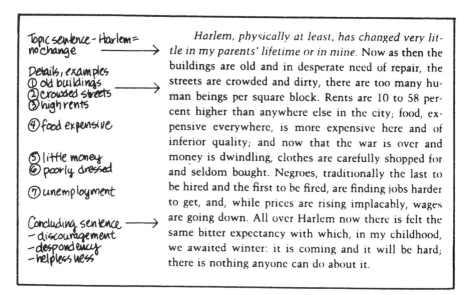

FIGURE 3.3 The Topic Sentence
Source: From Notes of a Native Son *by James Baldwin. Copyright © 1955, renewed 1983 by James Baldwin. Reprinted by permission of Beacon Press.*

1. Go back a couple of paragraphs to pick up the thread of the writer's ideas again.
2. Read ahead a couple of paragraphs to see where you're going.
3. Open your dictionary and look up any words that you are not sure of and that might be holding you back.
4. Reread the troublesome paragraph aloud, using exaggerated expression and emphasis to get at the meaning of what's being said. Such reading aloud, especially with expression, brings concentration back to a 100 percent level.

The Corson Technique.   Dale Corson, former president of Cornell University and dean of the College of Engineering, observed that engineers and other students in science and mathematics must often crack the meaning of an idea or concept one sentence at a time. If comprehension does not occur even at this snail's pace, then you must ask your instructor for help. "But before you do," says Dr. Corson, "ask yourself this question: What is it that I don't understand?"

Under no circumstance should you go to the instructor, open the book, and with a broad sweep of your hand say, "I don't understand this." When you go for help, you should be able to say, "I understand and follow the writer's idea up to this point and even beyond this point, but for some reason this particular section has no meaning for me." That way, the instructor knows not only what you understand and don't understand but also that you did your utmost to achieve understanding. You now have set the stage for a meaningful learning session.

The Corson Technique has a wonderful by-product. After analyzing and verbalizing your problem, after you have viewed it from several angles, you will most likely have solved it yourself. You may not have to discuss it with anyone else.

Additional Reading Strategies.   When you read sentences, make full use of signal words and organizational clues. If a sentence or paragraph begins "on the one hand," watch for the inevitable "on the other hand," which introduces the other side of the argument. Innocent little everyday words such as "since," "because," and "although" are as important in relating parts of a sentence as a plus, minus, or square-root sign is in a math equation. Ignoring or misreading them can get you into serious trouble.

If you get bogged down in a difficult sentence or paragraph, try reading the material without any modifying phrases. Find the simple subject of the sentence, the verb, and the simple object, to avoid getting lost in a maze of language. When the framework shows through clearly, so that you can grasp the main idea, then go back and read the material with all its "trimmings," to get its full sense.

After you finish a paragraph and summarize it, don't plunge immediately into the next paragraph. Pause for a minute or two, to think about the meaning of the paragraph you just read. Such a thinking pause provides time for the main idea to consolidate, to sink into your memory.

Whenever you encounter a difficult, unusual, or new word or term in your textbook, look it up in a glossary or dictionary. Put these words and terms, with their definitions, on 3 × 5 cards. You can learn these words and terms by carrying the cards and looking them over whenever you have a chance.

When you feel bored, do not reward your boredom by slamming your book shut and leaving empty-minded. Above all, don't reward yourself by going to a movie. If you get bored, give yourself the limited objective of extracting one nugget of knowledge, be it ever so small. Then, with that *accomplished*, you have *earned* the right to a break or a movie.

Step 4: Writing Questions in the Margins

The question-in-the-margin step is different in purpose from the question step of the SQ3R Method. In the SQ3R Method, the purpose of the question is to keep the reader alert, concentrating, and looking for an answer to the limited question that was asked. The question step of SQ3R directs the reader to turn headings and subheadings into questions. Obviously, putting "what" or "how" in front of a heading does not transform it automatically into a deep and searching question. A heading that is limited to begin with will remain limited after the addition of "what" or "how."

To be sure, this does not mean that the question step in SQ3R is not a good one. It serves a definite and valuable purpose when you are reading paragraphs or sections of the textbook for the first time. However, it is hard to imagine that you will be able to formulate a provocative question on textbook material before you have read, understood, and thought about the material. Merely asking a question before reading does not in any way guarantee that an answer will be forthcoming, regardless of how hard you read. Coming up with answers is not easy. Usually you have to dig hard for a comprehensive, accurate answer, and that is why the question-in-the-margin step comes into the system at this time—after you have read a paragraph thoroughly.

Once you have read a paragraph thoroughly and have been able to answer questions such as "What is the main idea here?" or "What are the important points made here?" you are ready to formulate and write a brief, telegraphic question in the margin of your textbook. After writing the question, you should then, for the first time, underline very sparingly only the key words and phrases that make up the answer. The less underlining you do, the better.

Later, when you review for an exam, your eyes and mind will be directed to the words and phrases that deliver the meaning directly and efficiently. When you underline only the key words and phrases, you have to think, and thinking is what makes understanding and remembering possible.

Go through the entire chapter in this way: reading thoroughly to understand the passage; writing a brief, meaningful question; and underlining sparingly. Figure 3.4 shows the questions-in-the-margin technique applied to a textbook page.

Step 5: Reciting Based on the Questions in the Margin

After formulating questions on the entire chapter, go back to the beginning of the chapter and cover the printed text with a blank sheet of paper, exposing only the questions you've written in the margin. Read the first question aloud, and answer the question in your own words. Slide the blank sheet down to check your answer. If your answer is wrong or incomplete, recite it aloud again. Do this until you get the answer right. Go through the entire chapter in this way. Your aim is to establish in your memory an accurate, crystal-clear impression, because that's what you want to return to later

---

WRITING GOOD PAPERS IN COLLEGE

What 2 aspects lead to success?

The techniques of writing a good paper are easy to follow. You should remember two important aspects that lead to success. First, start work early on the paper. Second, if you have a choice, choose a subject that you are interested in, or that you can develop an interest in.

What 3 elements might make up a paper?

Much of your work in college involves absorbing knowledge; when it comes to writing papers, you have the opportunity to put down on paper what you've learned about a subject, and perhaps your opinions and conclusions on the subject.

What's the key in choosing a topic?

Writing is an important form of communication. To communicate well you must have something you really want to say. So if you have a choice of topics, choose one that intrigues you. If it isn't one that everyone else is writing on, all the better. If you're not sure about your choice of topic, do a

If not sure of a topic, do what?

little preliminary research to see what's involved in several topics before you make a final decision. Remember the caution about allowing yourself enough time? Here's where it comes into play. Take enough time to choose a topic carefully (see Chapter 15 for specific pointers).

FIGURE 3.4   Writing Questions in the Margin

during an exam. If the impression in your memory is fuzzy at this time, it will be even fuzzier three or four weeks later.

Why Recite Aloud? Reciting aloud forces you to think, and it is this thinking that leaves behind in your memory a neural trace to come back to. You must believe, without an iota of doubt and without a moment of hesitation, that forgetting is and will continue to be your major academic problem. Forgetting erodes, corrodes, and thwarts learning. Forgetting never lets up. It works continuously to expel from memory what you worked so hard—often far into the night—to put there. Don't let forgetting get the upper hand. You can bring forgetting almost to a standstill by using the power of recitation.

Reciting promotes concentration, forms a sound basis for understanding the next paragraph or the next chapter, provides time for the memory trace to consolidate, ensures that facts and ideas are remembered accurately, and provides immediate feedback on how you're doing (and when you know that you're doing well, you will make progress). Moreover, experiments have shown that the greater the proportion of reciting time to reading time, the greater is the learning. Students who spent 20 percent of their time reading and 80 percent reciting did much better than students who spent less time reciting and more time reading.

When you recite aloud, don't mumble. Express the ideas in complete sentences, using the proper signal words. For example, when you are reciting a list of ideas or facts, enumerate them by saying "first," "second," and so on. Insert words such as "furthermore," "however," and "finally." When you do so in oral practice, you will do so most naturally in writing during an exam.

The New Way: Reciting and Visualizing. Visualizing is a powerful new technique for increasing your learning and your remembering. As you recite, instead of just mouthing the answer, picture yourself as a scholar-orator standing by your seat in the classroom reciting your answer to the instructor. Although you are actually sitting at your desk in your room and reciting in a lively manner, in your mind's eye you are standing in the classroom speaking, explaining, and gesturing.

Many successful athletes use visualization all the time. They burn such a positive image in their minds that it becomes part of the subconscious, and they expect the performance that they visualized to be carried out in actuality. Dwight Stones, a former U.S. Olympic high jumper, is very well known for the way in which he visualizes each jump before he actually makes it. There's nothing subtle about Stones. As he stands staring at the bar, his head bobs and you can almost visualize his jump yourself. His little routine might almost be comical except for one thing: Stones has won countless gold medals in international competition, and so instead of being laughed at for his peculiar routine, he is widely imitated by younger athletes who literally and figuratively are hoping to reach the heights that Stones has achieved.

Picture yourself in a classroom writing the answer to an essay question. Visualize the entire scene: the classroom, the other students, the instructor, the exam being handed out, your reading the questions. Now look at your textbook; read the question in the margin aloud; think for a few moments how you plan to organize and deliver your answer. Then, as if you were in an exam, recite softly to yourself and at the same time write your answer as you would if the exam were real. Try to *see* yourself in the classroom, thinking and writing forcefully and successfully. In this way you'll be creating in your brain cells a deep, well-defined pattern that will be easy to come back to and follow when the real exam is given. To learn more about how to think visually, see Pauk: *How to Study in College.*

Step 6: Reviewing Immediately and Later _____

Immediately after you have recited the whole chapter, you should finish the session with a general, relaxed overview, using the questions in the margins as cues. The purpose of the general overview is to put together all the separate questions and answers—to snap them together like the parts of a jigsaw puzzle and reveal the chapter as a whole.

This overview is made not by reciting the whole business over again—you've had enough of that for a while. Rather, look thoughtfully at each question in the margin, mentally glimpse the answer, and hold the answer in mind for a few seconds. Proceed through the entire chapter in this way. Don't make this process a chore. Actually, it could be a pleasant process, similar to taking a sweeping glance at a lawn you've finished mowing or a room you've straightened up. Take a last mental look at the questions and answers, and try to see the chapter as a whole.

The immediate review is important—very important—but it is not enough. You should review thoroughly and often. Later reviews should be conducted in the same way as the immediate review: using questions in the margins as cues, one page at a time, aloud, and in your own words. These later reviews will keep you in a state of preparedness for quizzes and exams. There will be no need to cram your head full of ideas and facts on the night before an exam. All you'll need is a refresher, in the same form—one more review.

As you review, look for ways to connect or categorize, to put like things together and to place opposite things opposite each other. Look for common characteristics, differences, or functions by which to categorize facts and ideas. This type of analysis puts you in control and gives you the chance to use your creativity—to bring the textbook to life and bring order to the mass of information you are required to learn. Categorizing also puts to practical use the Magical Number Seven Theory—the finding that the immediate memory seems to be limited to seven categories, which can be as broad as you care to make them.

The best time for a fast review of your textbook is the half hour before going to bed. Things learned then have a way of lingering in the conscious mind during the time before sleep comes and in the subconscious mind after sleep comes.

Step 7: Reflecting on Facts and Ideas

After you learn facts and ideas through recitation and immediate review, let your mind reflect on them. Let it speculate or play with the knowledge you've acquired. To engage in reflection is to bring creativity to your learning. Ask yourself such questions as these: What is the significance of these facts and ideas? What principle or principles are they based on? What else could they be applied to? How do they fit in with what I already know? From these facts and ideas, what else can I learn? When you reflect, you weave new facts and ideas into your existing knowledge. They then become part of your regular stock of thinking tools.

There's a huge difference between proficiency and creativity. You can become proficient by studying your textbooks and lecture notes, but you will never be creative until you try to see beyond the facts, to leap mentally beyond the given. You must reflect on the facts and ideas, because creativity comes only through reflection, not from recitation and review.

To survive academically in college, you have to recite. To grow in creativity and in wisdom, you have to reflect.

The Reciter . . .	*The Reflector . . .*
● Follows strictly the ideas and facts in the textbook	● Pursues ideas and facts through additional reading in the library and goes to original works
● Is bound by the course outline	● Uses the course outline as a point of departure
● Is diligent and disciplined in memorizing but keeps ideas and facts at arm's length	● Is adventuresome and experimental and internalizes facts and ideas
● Is so busy reciting that the framework of the course is vaguely seen or missed	● Is likely to see the framework of the course and to talk to the instructor because of ideas occurring during reflection

- Understands the literal meaning but not the implications of assignments
- Learns and accepts facts and ideas in the sequential order of the textbook

- Applies learning to various situations
- Thinks, hypothesizes, speculates, and then tests ideas independently

Use reflection often. Reflection is a skill you can take with you wherever you go and use in spare moments. You can reflect while walking from one building to another, standing in line, waiting for a friend, or riding a bus. People who have made great discoveries have reported that some of their best insights came in unlikely places and at odd times. A classic example is that of Archimedes (287?–212 B.C.), the greatest mathematician of ancient times, who discovered the natural law of buoyancy while taking a bath. He became so excited that he ran naked through the streets shouting, "Eureka!"

Begin with the facts and ideas you have learned, and become curious about them. Look at them in different ways, combine them, separate them into the basics, try to find out what would happen if the opposite were true, and so on. This may be difficult at first, but it will become easier as your creativity grows. Continue your reflection until your ideas take definite shape. Don't leave them vague. If you need more information, an encyclopedia or a standard source book on the subject will often help you bring fuzzy ideas into focus.

The only type of learning that becomes a permanent part of you and increases your innate wisdom is *advantageous learning*—learning that occurs when you take a voluntary, extra step beyond the mere memorization of facts. That extra step is reflection. In the words of the philosopher Arthur Schopenhauer (1788–1860): "A man may have a great mass of knowledge, but if he has not worked it up by thinking it over for himself, it has much less value than a far smaller amount which he has thoroughly pondered."

SUMMARY

What's the best way to get the semester off to a good start?

Buy all your books just as soon as you've registered, so that you will have time to read the table of contents, preface, introduction, and other up-front material in each textbook.

What good is the preface?

The preface is the one place where most authors drop their scholarly style. As a result, you may get a clear picture of the man or woman who has written your textbook. In addition, the preface provides information not available elsewhere: what the author's objective is and is not, how the book is organized, how and why the book is different from other books on the same subject, and the author's qualifications for writing the book.

With all that information in the preface, what's the point of the introduction?

Whereas the preface deals in matters broad and general, the author's introduction is often narrow and specific. From the introduction you'll learn the underlying principles of the book. Many students refer to the introduction before they tackle each new chapter, just to be sure that they're on the right track.

How does the SQ3R Method of study work?

In five steps—survey, question, read, recite, and review—the SQ3R Method helps you approach reading assignments systematically. First you survey the headings in a chapter and read the summary at the end. Then you turn these headings into questions. Read so as to answer that question, then look away from the book and briefly recite the answer you've found. Review your notes to get a bird's-eye view of all the points you've raised and their relationship to one another. SQ3R should result in faster reading and efficient learning.

How does the 3Rs System work?

The 3Rs System is for students who work well under the pressure of time and exams. The three steps—read, record, and recite—are simple and direct. First read several paragraphs, then return to the first paragraph and ask yourself what you need to know in the paragraph. Then underline key words, phrases, and sentences containing that information. Jot a brief question that asks for this underlined information. Cover the pages of your assignment and try to answer the questions you've posed in the margins. Recite in this way until you finish the chapter.

How does the Questions-in-the-Margin System work?

This technique combines the simplicity of the 3Rs System with the long-term effectiveness of SQ3R. It has seven clear and helpful steps.

What is the first step in the Questions-in-the-Margin System?

Before you begin to read a textbook assignment in earnest, survey, or skim, it first. The few minutes that you spend surveying a chapter can be invaluable.

Isn't surveying a waste of time?

No. Surveying a chapter can help you in at least four ways: (1) Surveying provides you with background information. (2) Surveying provides advance organizers—familiar landmarks that act as topics or categories around which you can cluster ideas, facts, and details. (3) Surveying readies your mind for the task of reading the textbook chapter. (4) Surveying overcomes mental inertia by easing you into a task (reading your textbook) that you might otherwise have put off.

What is the second step in the Questions-in-the-Margin System?

In the second step, you turn the chapter headings into questions, or you ask some general questions that can be applied to any topic. In either case, you suddenly have a purpose for reading. As a result, you don't simply stare at the words, you interact with them. Remember: Students who have *answers to give* when they finish reading are usually those who had *questions to ask* while they read.

What does the third step, reading paragraph by paragraph, entail?

When you begin to read a textbook chapter, it is crucial for you to understand one paragraph before you move on to the next. You should read and reread until you are able to answer the question "What did the author say in this paragraph?"

Is there a key to understanding the meaning of a paragraph?

Yes. The topic sentence of each paragraph generally contains the main idea or points to the main idea. It is often the first sentence in the paragraph.

What should I do if I can't make sense of a paragraph?

There are five techniques to get yourself out of a jam: (1) Go back a few paragraphs to pick up the thread of the author's ideas. (2) Read ahead a paragraph or two to see what's coming. (3) Grab a dictionary and look up any words that are acting as stumbling blocks. (4) Reread the troublesome paragraph out loud using exaggerated intonation to get at the meaning of the author's words. (5) If the first four techniques don't work, use the Corson Technique: Identify specifically what's causing you trouble. When you take pains to pinpoint a problem, you often wind up solving the problem. If you're still stumped, take your specific question to your instructor.

Are there any other ways to get a lot out of my reading?

Yes. Here are a few: (1) Be on the alert for signal words and organizational clues that tell you where the author is going. (2) To make sense of an especially complex sentence, simplify things by reading the material without any modifiers. (3) Pause after each paragraph so that your mind has a chance to absorb new information. (4) Transfer new and difficult words to 3×5 cards, where they can be studied and mastered so that you won't have to look them up again. (5) If you begin to lose interest in your reading, instead of closing the book and giving up, make an effort to extract at least one more piece of information before you move on to something else.

How does step 4, writing questions in the margins, differ from step 2?

In step 2 you were asked to formulate questions primarily to keep you alert and to keep you reading. When you have read a paragraph carefully and thoroughly, you should

	be able to ask deep and meaningful questions about it—the kind of questions that you are likely to find on an exam. Once you've written a question in the margin, go back to the text itself and underline the key words and terms that aid in answering your question.
Is there any point in going beyond step 4? Isn't writing questions in the margin the way to gain important information?	If you want to remember information, you must recite it. When you have formulated questions for the entire chapter, go back over the text and read your questions aloud one at a time, answering them correctly before you move on. Reciting out loud forces you to think while you recite and helps keep forgetting in check.
How do I apply step 6, reviewing?	Begin with an immediate review. As soon as you've finished reciting a chapter, take a moment to look over your notes in an effort to pull things together in your mind. Formulating the "big picture" improves the likelihood that the facts from the chapter will remain in your memory.
How do I go about reflecting?	Begin by questioning the things you learn. Wonder about their significance, the principles on which they are based, and other ideas they might be applied to. In short, try to see beyond the facts and ideas in the pages of your textbooks.

HAVE YOU MISSED SOMETHING?

1. *Sentence completion.*   Complete the following sentences with one of the three words listed below each sentence.

    a. Frequent and thorough reviews help to eliminate the need for ____.

      recitation   cramming   reflection

    b. When you use the Questions-in-the-Margin System, you should underline the textbook _____.

      sparingly   frequently   initially

    c. Learning is most likely to occur when the proportion of reciting time to reading time is _____.

    high   equal   low

2. *Matching.* In each blank space in the left column, write the number preceding the phrase in the right column that matches the left item best.

____ a. Reflection	1. Time-honored way to study textbooks
____ b. 3Rs System	2. Pinpoints what you don't understand
____ c. Recitation	3. Reveals author's objectives
____ d. Review	4. Brings creativity to learning
____ e. Preface	5. Step not found in the 3Rs System
____ f. SQ3R Method	6. A three-step study method
____ g. Corson Technique	7. A powerful weapon for combating forgetting
____ h. Visualization	8. Adds a new dimension to the learning process

3. *True-false.* Write *T* beside the *true* statements and *F* beside the *false* statements.

    ____ a. The first few pages of a textbook should usually be skipped.

    ____ b. The Questions-in-the-Margin System has seven steps.

    ____ c. Surveying a chapter provides advance organizers.

    ____ d. Visualization will weaken the power of recitation.

    ____ e. Answers to questions in the margin may be written as well as recited.

4. *The preface.* Write "yes" next to the common characteristics of a textbook preface.

    ____ a. Tells what the author's objective is

    ____ b. Deals with matters narrow and specific

    ____ c. Explains why the book is different from other books on the same subject

    ____ d. Serves as a guide for upcoming chapters

_____ e. Tells what the author's objective is not

_____ f. Presents the organizational plan of the book

5. *Multiple choice.*   Choose the word that completes the following sentence most accurately, and circle the letter that precedes it.

    The Questions-in-the-Margin System ultimately aids your mind's ability to

    a. recall
    b. recognize
    c. reflect
    d. rephrase

CHAPTER

4

Answering True-False, Multiple-Choice, and Matching Questions

To be able to discern what is true is true and what is false is false; this is the mark and character of intelligence.

Emanuel Swedenborg (1688–1772), Swedish scientist, inventor, and theologian

Do you know right from wrong? Can you recognize a correct answer when you see one? This chapter will help you do both—on tests and exams. It tells you

- What to look for in true-false questions
- How to analyze multiple-choice questions
- How to work through matching questions

True-false questions, multiple-choice questions, and matching questions provide a very efficient way to test a student's knowledge of facts. With these types of questions, a fifty-minute test can cover a great deal of ground. Such questions are easy to grade, and the results depend only on knowledge; the student's writing ability doesn't get in the way of his or her answers.

The three types of questions are similar in one respect: The correct answer is provided; the student must identify it. In spite of this similarity, different techniques are used to analyze and answer true-false, multiple-choice, and matching questions.

WHAT TO LOOK FOR IN TRUE-FALSE QUESTIONS

In its simplest form, a true-false question is a statement that attributes a property or quality to one or more persons or things:

T F   Birds can fly.

T F   Students are creative.

T F   Snakes are poisonous.

In the first statement, the ability to fly is attributed to (or connected with) birds. In the second, the quality of creativeness is connected with students. In the third, the property of being poisonous is attributed to snakes. On an exam you would circle *T* in all three cases, because all three statements are true. There are birds that can fly; there are students who are creative; and there are snakes that are poisonous. You should have no trouble with such simple, straightforward statements. The problem is that very few (if any) true-false statements are written so simply. Most contain qualifiers, negatives, or strings of qualities that make them more difficult to handle.

Watch Out for Qualifiers _____

Here's what happens when we add *qualifiers* to our basic true-false questions:

T F   *All* birds can fly.

T F   *Some* students are creative.

T F   *Most* snakes are poisonous.

In each case, one small word—the qualifier—makes a big difference in the basic statement.

The first statement, "All birds can fly," is false, because birds such as the ostrich and the penguin cannot fly. The qualifier *all* overstates the connection between birds and flying. The second statement is true because *some* students are indeed creative. The qualifier *some* does not overstate or understate the situation. The third statement, "Most snakes are poisonous," is false; of the three thousand different kinds of land snakes, only about 250 are poisonous. Here again the qualifier leads to overstatement.

Qualifiers may be grouped into sets. The six most-used sets are

All—Most—Some—None (No)

Always—Usually—Sometimes—Never

Great—Much—Little—No

More—Equal—Less

Good—Bad

Is—Is Not

Within each set, the qualifiers may overstate a true-false statement, understate it, or make it just right. Memorize the six sets. They will help you answer many true-false questions.

Whenever one qualifier from a set is used in a true-false statement, substitute each of the others for it, in turn. In this way, determine which of the qualifiers in the set fits best (makes the statement just right). If that is the given qualifier, the answer is *true;* otherwise, the answer is *false.*

For example, suppose you are given the question

T   F   All birds can fly.

Substituting the other qualifiers in the "all" set gives you these four statements:

All birds can fly.

Most birds can fly.

Some birds can fly.

No birds can fly.

The statement beginning with the word *most* is just right, but that is not the statement you were given. Therefore, the answer is *false.*

Some qualifiers are "100 percent words." They imply that the statements they appear in are true 100 percent of the time. These words are

No	Every	Only
Never	Always	Entirely
None	All	Invariably
		Best

Such qualifiers are almost always connected with a false statement, because there are very few things in this world that are 100 percent one way or the other. Here are two examples:

All chickens make clucking sounds.

No true chicken can swim.

Always watch out for these qualifying words, but don't automatically consider a statement wrong simply because it contains one of them. To keep you honest and alert, some instructors will occasionally use them in true statements:

All stars are surrounded by space.

All human beings need food to survive.

No human being can live without air.

Qualifying words that fall between the extremes are generally used in true statements. Here are some in-between qualifiers:

Seldom	Most	Usually
Sometimes	Many	Generally
Often	Few	Ordinarily
Frequently	Some	

Here are two items in which these words are used:

T   F   *Many* birds fly south for the winter.

T   F   A balanced diet *usually* leads to better health.

To test your ability to recognize and work with qualifiers, do the exercise in Figure 4.1.

Check Each Part of the Statement _____

If any part of a true-false statement is false, then the whole statement is false. Be suspicious of a statement that contains a string of items, but don't conclude that it is false only because it contains the string. Here are two examples of statements with strings:

A long-term sales chart shows the dollar sales and sales trend by weeks, months, and years.

A warm-climate product, cocoa is grown in the Gold Coast of Africa, Nigeria, Brazil, Colombia, Venezuela, and in southern Norway.

The first statement is true because a long-term sales chart does show both dollar sales and the sales trend, which is indicated by the up-and-down

The following quiz, specifically designed both for students who have had a course in psychology and for those who have not, illustrates the importance of key words in objective questions. Take the quiz, picking out the key words and writing them in the space provided. In most cases, there is only one key word, but in a few instances, there are two or three. Also indicate in the right-hand column whether you think the statement is true or false. When you are finished, look below for the correct answers.

1. Geniuses are usually queerer than people of average intelligence. _____ __
2. Only human beings, not animals, have the capacity to think. _____ __
3. Much of human behavior is instinctive. _____ __
4. Slow learners remember what they learn better than fast learners. _____ __
5. Intelligent people form most of their opinions by logical reasoning. _____ __
6. A psychologist is a person who is trained to psychoanalyze people. _____ __
7. You can size up a person very well in an interview. _____ __
8. When one is working for several hours, it is better to take a few long rests than several short ones. _____ __
9. The study of mathematics exercises the mind so that a person can think more logically in other subjects. _____ __
10. Grades in college have little to do with success in business careers. _____ __
11. Alcohol, taken in small amounts, is a stimulant. _____ __
12. There is a clear distinction between the normal person and one who is mentally ill. _____ __
13. Prejudices are mainly due to lack of information. _____ __
14. Competition among people is characteristic of most human societies. _____ __
15. The feature of a job that is most important to employees is the pay they get for their work. _____ __
16. It is possible to classify people very well into introverts and extroverts. _____ __
17. Punishment is usually the best way of eliminating undesirable behavior in children. _____ __
18. By watching closely a person's expression, you can tell quite well the emotion he is experiencing. _____ __
19. The higher one sets his goals in life, the more he is sure to accomplish and the happier he will be. _____ __
20. If a person is honest with you, he usually can tell you what his motives are. _____ __

ANSWERS FOR EXERCISE IN KEY WORDS

The key words for each question were as follows: (1) usually, (2) only, not, (3) much, (4) better, (5) most, (6) psychoanalyze, (7) very well, (8) better, (9) in other subjects, (10) little, (11) stimulant, (12) clear, (13) mainly, (14) most, (15) most important, (16) very well, (17) usually, best, (18) quite well, (19) sure, happier, (20) usually. All the statements are false. The reasons for their being false can be found in the book from which they were taken or, very likely, in any general course in psychology.

FIGURE 4.1   An Exercise in Key Words (Qualifiers)
Source: Clifford T. Morgan, Introduction to Psychology, *copyright 1961. Reprinted by permission of McGraw-Hill Publishing Company.*

movement of the graph. In addition, the time scale on the chart is marked in weeks and months as well as years.

The first nineteen words of the second statement are true. The last two words, "southern Norway," are false because cocoa grows only in warm climates—and Norway, both northern and southern, is freezing cold in winter. This one false item makes the entire statement false.

Some tricky (and usually false) statements are made up of two "substatements," both of which may be true. The two substatements are connected by a conjunction such as *therefore, thus, because, consequently,* or *so,* or a phrase such as *as a result.* What generally makes the statement false is that the second substatement doesn't logically follow from the first. In other words, the two parts are not directly related, although the statement is presented as if they are. For example, consider this statement:

> Thomas Edison invented the ticker-tape machine for recording stock prices and, *as a result,* he became famous.

It is true that Edison invented the ticker-tape machine and that he became famous in his lifetime. However, his fame was due not directly to his ticker-tape machine but to other inventions, including the electric light bulb, the phonograph, and the storage battery. For this reason, the statement is false.

Beware of the Negative

True-false statements that contain negative words and prefixes are difficult to sort out and answer. The negatives can upset or complicate your thinking. Negative words include *not* and *cannot,* and the negative prefixes are *dis-, il-, im-, in-, ir-, non-,* and *un-,* as in *inconsequential* or *illogical.*

Notice, in the following three statements, how the addition of negatives increases the difficulty of understanding what the statements mean—let alone deciding whether they are true or false.

> Thomas Edison's fame was due to his many practical inventions.

> It is illogical to assume that Thomas Edison's fame was due to his many practical inventions.

> It is illogical to assume that Thomas Edison's fame was not due to his many practical inventions.

When you are confronted with such a statement, begin by circling the negative words and negative prefixes. Then try to get the meaning of the statement without the negatives. Finally, reread the sentence to find out whether it is true or false in its entirety. Here, the first statement is true, the second is false, and the third is true.

Think "True"—and Guess When You Must _____

Most true-false tests contain more true statements than false statements, simply because they are made up by teachers. Since teachers would rather leave true information in your mind, they tend to stack the test with true statements. Of course, some teachers will fool you, but after the first test you'll know for sure.

On a true-false test, it is a good idea to guess at answers that you don't know, even if credit is subtracted for wrong answers. According to the laws of probability, you should get 50 percent right when you guess, even if you know nothing about the subject matter. If you can make intelligent guesses—knowing that there are more true than false statements—you should be able to do much better than that.

HOW TO ANALYZE MULTIPLE-CHOICE QUESTIONS

Most multiple-choice questions[1] are of the incomplete-statement type. A partial statement (called the *stem*) leads grammatically into four or five sentence endings, or options, listed directly under it. One of the options is the correct answer. The other (incorrect) options are called *distractors* or *decoys*.

Here is an example of a well-constructed multiple-choice question:

Stem ————→   1. The almost perfect walls of granite boulders surrounding some lakes in Iowa were formed by
           a. American Indians
Decoys   b. prehistoric men
Correct   c. huge meteors
Answer   d. thick ice

This incomplete-statement question exhibits good construction in the following ways:

1. All options are grammatically consistent.

2. The stem is long, and the options are short.

3. Extraneous material is excluded from the stem.

_____

[1]Some of the ideas in this section were inspired by James F. Shepherd, *The Houghton Mifflin Study Skills Handbook* (Boston: Houghton Mifflin, 1982), pp. 230–70.

4. The stem contains one central problem.

5. Double negatives are not used.

6. All options are plausible.

7. The correct option is no longer or shorter than the others.

8. Only one option is the correct or best answer.[2]

When the use of an incomplete statement would lead to an awkward stem or options, the question form is used, and the options are listed below the question.

Answering Multiple-Choice Questions _____

Before you even look at a question on a multiple-choice test, you must *read the directions carefully.* Some say, "Mark the one best answer," whereas others may require that you "Mark all correct answers." You will lose credit if you mark more than one answer in the first case, or if you miss a correct option in the second case. If the directions are not clear, then *ask.*

Begin each question by reading the stem all the way through. Then read the options all the way through. Don't be in a rush to mark the first option that sounds good. In some questions, *all* the options may be correct, and you have to choose the best one; you won't find it unless you read them all.

You should read all the options even when the question seems unfamiliar. One of them might provide you with a hint as to what the question is about. Furthermore, there's information in the options themselves—information that might help you remember what you need to know.

After you read the stem and the options, spend no more than a few seconds puzzling over the question. If it resists answering, cross out any options you have eliminated, mark the question so you will be able to find it easily later, and move on to the next question. But don't leave any question so fast that you do not give it the calm consideration it deserves. If you merely go through the motions, you're wasting time. The idea is to convert the easy questions into quick point-getters and leave enough time to go back to the questions you skipped.

When you have worked your way through the test, go back to the questions that you marked for reconsideration. This time, however, concentrate on eliminating options. The more distractors you can eliminate, the better your chance of finding the correct answer.

---

[2]William D. Hedges, "How to Construct a Good Multiple-Choice Test," *The Clearing House* 39 (September 1964): 9–11.

If you can somehow eliminate all the distractors, then you will have isolated the correct answer. If you can eliminate only one or two of the options, then you should guess at the correct answer. In the long run you will come out ahead by doing so, even if some credit is subtracted for each incorrect answer.

Here are some additional hints that may be of help to you in eliminating distractors and choosing the correct answer.

Try to Apply the True-False Technique

To use the true-false technique, you make a complete statement from the stem and each option, in turn. An option that results in a false statement is eliminated as a distractor. One that results in a true statement is probably the correct answer. As an example, consider this multiple-choice question:

2. Because of its lack of lumber, Syria has many "beehive" homes built of
   a.   metal
   b.   concrete
   c.   marble
   d.   mud brick

To judge the correctness of the first option, you would complete the stem as follows: Because of its lack of lumber, Syria has many "beehive" homes built of metal. Because Syria is a hot, dry, and rather poor country, you would probably decide that this statement is false. Metal (and concrete and marble as well) are too expensive and not readily available to the vast majority of people. The last option, *mud brick,* undoubtedly produced locally, would be inexpensive and available and would hold up in a country where rainfall is meager. (The correct answer is *d.*)

When you use this technique, don't be too quick to eliminate options; do so only after sufficient consideration. If you have eliminated three options but don't like the remaining option, you must go back and reconsider them all.

Stick to the Subject Matter of the Course

When a multiple-choice question includes options that you don't recognize or that seem out of place, don't get panicked into choosing one of them. The chances are great that the strange options are distractors. Here's an example:

3. Which of the following does not have satellites (moons)?
   a.   Venus
   b.   Cassiopeia
   c.   Mars
   d.   Perseus

You might reason as follows: "We've been studying planets and their rotation around the sun. I've heard of Cassiopeia, but we haven't studied it. I've never heard of Perseus. I bet both are decoys—I'll cross them off. We did study Venus and Mars. They are planets, but I don't remember which one has satellites and which one doesn't. Well, at least I've boiled things down to a fifty-fifty chance. I'll mark this question and come back to it later."

Later, when you return to the question, you might remember that Mars has a ring of satellites or moons around it. That would eliminate Mars, leaving Venus. You still might not remember whether Venus has satellites, but since that's the only option left, you would choose it. (*Venus* is the correct answer.)

Watch Out for Negatives and Extreme Words

We discussed negatives and extreme words in relation to true-false questions, and our discussion applies here as well. Whenever you find negative words such as *not* or *except* in the stem or in the options, circle them so they'll stand out. Then make sure you take them into consideration when you choose your answer. Here's an example:

4. Which materials are (not) used in making saddles?
   a.   linen, canvas, serge
   b.   wood and leather
   c.   rubber and cork
   d.   iron and steel

(The correct answer is *d*. The materials in *a, b,* and *c* are all used in saddles.)

Always circle 100 percent words such as *never, no, none, best, worst, always, all,* and *every;* and be suspicious of the options in which you find them. In fact, if you have to guess, first eliminate all the options that contain absolute words. Then choose your answer from the remaining options. As an example, see whether you can answer this question:

5. The author suggests that the desert
   a.   climate is unpredictable
   b.   heat is always unbearable

c. is totally devoid of rain

d. earthquakes pose a constant danger

You should have circled *always* in *b, totally* in *c,* and *constant* in *d,* to obtain *a* as the correct answer. You didn't even have to know what the question is about.

Foolish Options Are Usually Incorrect _____

Test writers occasionally include a silly statement as an option. Most likely, they become tired and simply dash off foolish statements to fill space. You should almost always view such statements as distractors worthy of being immediately crossed out. Here's an example:

6. The most important reason why the travel agents tested the Camel Caravan was to

a. judge the safety aspects of the trip

b. improve relations with the Arabs

c. get a free vacation

d. test the appeal of the Caravan for tourists

The foolish option is *c.* The correct option is *d.* Notice that options *a* and *b* make true statements, but the word *most* in the stem calls for option *d.*

The Option "All the Above" Is Usually Correct _____

When all the reasonable candidates for options will make the statement true, test writers frequently use "all the above" as an option. Doing so greatly simplifies the writing of such a question. Here's an example:

7. Until the first half of the second millennium B.C., an army laying siege to a city made use of

a. scaling ladders

b. siege towers

c. archery fire

d. all the above

(The correct option is *d.*)

One way to confirm the choice "all the above" is to find two correct answers in the options. For example, suppose you were sure that ladders and towers were used, but you weren't sure about archery fire. Then, if only one answer were permitted, that answer would have to be *d,* because *d* is the only option that includes *a* and *b.*

Numbers in the Middle Range Are Usually Correct ___

When all the options in a multiple-choice question are numbers, the answer is easy if you have memorized the correct number. Otherwise, you'll probably have to do some guessing. If you have no other information to go on, your chances of guessing correctly are increased if you eliminate the highest and lowest numbers. For some reason, test writers usually include at least one number lower than the correct answer and at least one number higher than the correct answer. This "rule" allows you to eliminate half of the options in the following example:

8. The "Great Pyramid" originally stood how many feet high?
   a. 281
   b. 381
   c. 481
   d. 981

You would eliminate 281 as the lowest number and 981 as the highest, leaving two middle-range numbers, 381 and 481. At this point you have a fifty-fifty chance of choosing correctly. Can you improve the odds?

You could compare the two remaining options to something you know, such as a football field. Then, 381 feet is slightly greater than a football field, perhaps not so high for a pyramid. But 481 feet is over 1½ times as high as a football field is long. That would really make a "Great Pyramid." (If you stuck with 481 feet, you would be correct.)

Check for Look-Alike Options ___

Test makers occasionally include, in one question, two options that are alike except for one word. Such a pair seems to indicate where the test maker's interest was focused, so it is logical to assume that one of the pair is the correct answer. The other options should, of course, be read carefully; they should be eliminated in favor of the look-alikes only in a guessing situation. For example, consider the question:

9. The author considers himself an authority on
   a. touring the Middle East
   b. Middle East rug dealers
   c. Middle East rug bargains
   d. behavior patterns of tourists

Even if you had no inkling of the correct answer, you would be wise to eliminate *a* and *d* and choose from the similar pair *b* and *c*. (The correct option is *b*.)

The test writer can keep you from using this technique by inserting two pairs of similar options. Then you would have to deal with four options:

10. The author considers himself an authority on
   a.   behavior patterns of merchants
   b.   Middle East rug dealers
   c.   Middle East rug bargains
   d.   behavior patterns of tourists

Check for Longer or More Inclusive Options _____

In multiple-choice questions, the correct option is often longer or more inclusive of qualities or ideas than the distractors. The length or inclusiveness results when the test writer must qualify or amplify a simple statement. So, be alert for a tightly packed or overly long option, as in this question:

11. The author says that rug buying in the Middle East is like courtship in that
   a.   both parties fool each other
   b.   both parties must trust each other
   c.   both parties desire the same thing but begin with expressions of disinterest
   d.   in rug buying, as in courtship, one dresses in one's best

(Here option *c* is correct.)

HOW TO WORK THROUGH MATCHING QUESTIONS

Matching questions provide a most efficient way to test knowledge in courses such as history (in which events, dates, names, and places are important) and psychology (for which numerous experiments, experimenters, results, and special terms and definitions have to be remembered). In a matching question, two vertical lists of items are placed next to each other. Each list contains a half dozen or more words or phrases, in random order. The task is to match the items in one list with those in the other list, according to a relation that is given in the directions for answering the question.

Figure 4.2 contains a matching question that will test your knowledge of inventors and their inventions. You may want to try it now, before you read the next section.

Match the inventions in the right-hand column with the inventors in the left-hand column by writing the proper letter in the space provided alongside each inventor's name. Use each item in the right-hand column only once.

Inventor	*Invention*
_____ 1. Eli Whitney	a. Automobile assembly line
_____ 2. James Watt	b. Telephone
_____ 3. Robert Fulton	c. Vulcanizing of rubber
_____ 4. Cyrus McCormick	d. Six-shooter revolver
_____ 5. Elias Howe	e. Steel plow
_____ 6. Henry Ford	f. Steamboat
_____ 7. James Hargreaves	g. Motion pictures
_____ 8. Richard Arkwright	h. Cotton gin
_____ 9. Samuel Colt	i. Dynamite
_____ 10. Charles Goodyear	j. Steam engine
_____ 11. Alfred Nobel	k. Telegraph
_____ 12. Thomas Edison	l. Sewing machine
_____ 13. Guglielmo Marconi	m. Spinning frame (textiles)
_____ 14. John Deere	n. Radio
_____ 15. Samuel Morse	o. Spinning jenny
_____ 16. Alexander Bell	p. Grain-reaping machine
	q. Locomotive (train)

Answers: (1) *h*, (2) *j*, (3) *f*, (4) *p*, (5) *l*, (6) *a*, (7) *o*, (8) *m*, (9) *d*, (10) *c*, (11) *i*, (12) *g*, (13) *n*, (14) *e*, (15) *k*, (16) *b*.

FIGURE 4.2 Matching: Inventors and Inventions

How to Answer a Matching Question _____

The following sequence of steps will help you work through any matching questions systematically and efficiently.

1. Read the directions. Then run your eyes down both columns to get a brief overview of the specific items you will be working with.

2. Read the top item in the left-hand column. Then look carefully and thoughtfully down the right-hand column until you find a match for it. Don't stop at the first likely match; instead, continue through to the end of the right-hand column, to make sure there is not a better match. (If the right-hand column has the longer entries, you can save reading time by looking for the matches in the left-hand column.)

3. When you are certain that you have found a match, fill in the proper letter or number. (If you match the wrong items, you'll not only lose credit on that match, but you will run into more trouble later.) If you're not sure, skip the item and come back to it.

Match the activities in the right-hand column with the names in the left-hand column by writing the proper letter in the space provided alongside each name. Use each item in the right-hand column only once.

Names	Activity
____ 1. Jesse Owens	a. Tennis
____ 2. Pete Rose	b. Swimming
____ 3. Joe Montana	c. Hockey
____ 4. Kareem Abdul-Jabbar	d. Aviation
____ 5. Wayne Gretzky	e. Basketball
____ 6. Althea Gibson	f. Movies
____ 7. Gertrude Ederle	g. Football
____ 8. Amelia Earhart	h. Opera
____ 9. Meryl Streep	i. Baseball
____ 10. Beverly Sills	j. Boxing
____ 11. Joe Louis	k. Track
	l. Soccer

Answers: (1) *k*, (2) *i*, (3) *g*, (4) *e*, (5) *c*, (6) *a*, (7) *b*, (8) *d*, (9) *f*, (10) *h*, (11) *j*.

FIGURE 4.3 Matching: Personalities

4. This is the secret: Continue down the left column, filling in all the matches *that you're sure of*. This will drastically and immediately reduce the number of items that are left when you have to make the more difficult matches. And the fewer the items, the better are your chances of being correct.

5. As you use each item in the right column, circle its letter or number to show that it has been used. (You may also want to add the number or letter of the item with which it has been matched. This keying of your matches will help you check your answers later.)

Don't do any guessing until you are almost absolutely sure you're completely stumped. If you make an incorrect match too soon, you'll remove a "live" item from later consideration; then a second match, which would have made use of that item, will also be wrong. So first do your very best; then, using common sense and hunches, go ahead and guess at the remaining matches.

In case you're not an expert on inventions, Figure 4.3 contains a matching question that features famous personalities of the past and present. If you didn't use the matching-question sequence for Figure 4.2, try it here.

How to Study for Matching Questions _____

If you know that your instructor includes a long matching question in almost every exam, here's the best way to prepare for it. As you read and mark your textbook, be alert for facts and ideas that are associated with people's names. On a separate sheet, list the names and facts opposite each other, so that you end up with two distinct vertical columns, as in the following example:

Names	Facts or Ideas	(Subject)
Susan B. Anthony	Women's movement	(Sociology)
Jack London	*Call of the Wild*	(Literature)
George Washington Carver	Agricultural chemist	(Science)
Lewis & Clark	American explorers	(History)
George A. Miller	Magic number seven	(Psychology)
William James	Pragmatism	(Philosophy)
Mozart	*Marriage of Figaro*	(Music)

To master your list, cover the fact column with a sheet of paper. Look at each item in the name column, and recite and write the corresponding fact or idea. Then, to make sure that you learn the material both ways, block out the name column and use the facts as your cues. The example given here includes items from various subject areas. The same steps can be taken in any single subject area.

SUMMARY

What makes some true-false questions so hard to answer?

The difficulty often occurs when the test maker uses qualifying words such as *all, most, some,* and *none.* You must know not only the main fact, but also whether the qualifying word overstates or understates the fact, making the statement false. Be especially watchful for words that allow no exceptions—that is, words such as *never, all, always, none,* and *every.* These words can change an otherwise true statement into a false one.

What if half of the statement is true and half is false?

Then the statement is false. Always judge the entire statement. Be especially careful when a statement contains a long list of items.

What else should I watch out for?

Watch out for negative and extreme words within the statement. To make sure you take them into consideration, begin your analysis of the question by drawing a circle around every negative word and prefix.

Should I guess on true-false tests?

Yes. You have a fifty-fifty chance of being right, and knowing something about the subject matter should give you the winning edge.

How should I answer multiple-choice questions?

Begin by reading the directions carefully. Then read each question carefully—both stem and options. Eliminate options (distractors) where you can. Try to use the options as clues, and try the true-false technique.

Should I answer each question before moving on?

No. Don't waste time on a question that you can't answer in a reasonable amount of time. Instead, cross out the options you have eliminated, mark the question so you can come back to it later, and go on to the next question.

What should I do when I return to a multiple-choice question?

Concentrate on eliminating distractors. Make full use of probability techniques by looking for foolish options, "all the above," and look-alike and long options. Guess when you are able to eliminate at least one option in a four-option question or two options in a five-option question.

What's the best way to work a matching question?

First read the instructions and all the listed items. Then mark only the matches you are sure of, one by one. Next, go back to the items that you have skipped, and try to match them. Guess only when you're completely stumped.

Why can I study for matching questions but not for the others?	You *can* study for all types of questions, but you can do some special studying for matching questions by making a list of likely matches and then learning your list.

HAVE YOU MISSED SOMETHING?

1. *Sentence completion.*   Complete the following sentences with one of the three words listed below each sentence.

   a.   Negative and absolute words should be _____.

   avoided   circled   defined

   b.   In matching questions, the fewer the remaining choices, the better are your chances of being _____.

   incorrect   correct   alert

2. *Matching.*   In each blank space in the left column, write the number preceding the phrase in the right column that matches the left item best.

   _____ a. Stem

   _____ b. Qualifier

   _____ c. Guessing

   _____ d. Distractor

   _____ e. Overstatement

   _____ f. Understatement

   1. Incorrect multiple-choice option
   2. Risk of the word *none*
   3. Correct option makes it a true statement
   4. Risk of the word *all*
   5. A word like *usually* or *some*
   6. A last resort for matching questions

3. *True-false.*   Write *T* beside the *true* statements and *F* beside the *false* statements.

   _____ a. Qualifiers make true-false statements easy to answer.

   _____ b. Complicated true-false statements are usually false.

   _____ c. Guessing is advised when you don't know the answer to a multiple-choice question.

   _____ d. In a well-constructed multiple-choice question, the correct option is always the shortest.

   _____ e. In a matching question, answers you've used should be circled or marked in some fashion.

_____ f. In a matching question, you should immediately guess at matches you are unsure about.

4. *Multiple choice.* Choose the phrase that completes the following sentence most accurately, and circle the letter that precedes it.

In a multiple-choice question, an option is usually correct if it is

a. longer and more inclusive than the other options
b. one of two look-alike options
c. the only nonabsolute option
d. all the above

CHAPTER
5

Psychology
and Careers

John P. Fiore, University of Illinois

"What can I do with a major in psychology? My friends tell me you can't do anything with a degree in psychology!"

Almost everyone who has taught psychology has heard these comments. Psychology is a popular major and minor and can lead to a broad range of jobs and career possibilities. Psychology courses, chosen as electives, provide effective support for numerous other careers. Nevertheless, discussing psychology careers in general terms is difficult. Psychologists trained in one area of specialization within the field may find a wide-open job market with an excellent salary potential, while those specializing in another area might encounter limited opportunities and comparatively low salaries. Career opportunities in some psychology specializations require a master's degree; career opportunities in others require a doctorate. Students considering a career in psychology should therefore examine their own interests, values, and goals in addition to job requirements and career potential in the field.

PSYCHOLOGY FOR NONPSYCHOLOGISTS

On many college campuses, psychology course enrollments are among the highest of any field. Many majors include required or recommended psychology courses, and psychology is among the more popular electives. Although not everyone should major or minor in psychology, the study of human behavior has applications to many careers outside of psychology including teaching, sales, industrial engineering, law, medicine, advertising, and careers in the business fields. Management, for example, is a field for which psychology provides a valuable background. While training in psychology is not necessarily training for management roles, some areas of psychological study—judgment, decision making, group dynamics, leadership, motivation, conflict, and perception—do apply directly to management careers.

Many students who have not chosen a major or who are unsure of their selection are concerned that they will make a wrong choice that will limit their career options. Some graduate or professional programs do require specific courses for admission and may even require students who lack a particular background to spend an extra semester or two taking foundation courses. But professional and graduate school programs seek the best students, regardless of undergraduate major. Many programs have no specific requirements for admission except minimum grade-point average and adequate entrance test scores. Psychology majors have found virtually every kind of graduate and professional programs open to them: business, law, medicine, mathematics, architecture, accounting, public health, and a host of other fields.

LEARNING BY DOING

In addition to taking relevant courses, students can learn about psychology through first-hand experience. Many students find summer and part-time jobs in settings that employ psychologists. Others obtain internships, which are available in various settings and are often offered through colleges and universities. Interns are usually paid and sometimes receive college credit for their experience. Both employment and internship positions provide an opportunity to observe and learn about what goes on in a setting where psychologists are practicing their profession.

Students can also gain experience through volunteer work. For example, by volunteering to assist faculty in their research, students can get a close view of a research career while also learning about the topic of the research project. After identifying offices, agencies, and people in related areas of interest, students can ask to help a few hours a week to learn more about the field. Agencies in some career areas—most noticeably in health care and mental health—have not only established formal volunteer programs but have also come to depend on a steady stream of volunteers.

Finally, informational interviewing is another good way to increase your knowledge about careers. Suggested by career development experts, this strategy involves contacting working professionals and asking about their jobs and career experiences. Many college and university career centers and some psychology student organizations and honor societies provide contact with alumni who agree to participate in informational interviewing with current students.

The experiences recommended here will not only provide a sound basis for choosing a career but will also help convince a graduate admission committee that a student is enthusiastic and committed.

PREPARATION FOR GRADUATE SCHOOL

Although some psychology jobs are open to people with a bachelor's degree, most jobs in psychology—especially those involving research—require a graduate degree. Psychology departments design programs like the following to prepare interested students for graduate school.

SAMPLE PROGRAM
Psychology Courses: introductory, statistics, research methods, at least two from the following courses: social, developmental, abnormal, personality; two of the following: biological, learning, cognitive, perception and sensory processes; advanced course work spread over two or three broad areas such as social, cognitive, biological, psychometrics, developmental, and clinical.

DECIDING ON AN AREA OF SPECIALIZATION

Before applying to graduate school, students must decide on a particular area of specialization. A student who wants to become a clinical psychologist, for example, must apply to a graduate program in that specialty. This does not mean that students must specialize as undergraduates. Graduate school admissions committees are interested in applicants with a strong basic background and a broad knowledge in the field. The graduate program itself will develop the specialists.

Nonetheless, some students will identify an area of interest early in their college career and will elect courses and related projects most relevant to those interests. In some cases, a university may offer a program in a particular branch of applied psychology, for example, and a student who has already chosen a career in that branch will not want to delay training. Frequently, students complete an applied undergraduate program to prepare for bachelor level jobs so that they might gain experience used to decide if they enjoy the area sufficiently to pursue a graduate degree. Before selecting an applied undergraduate program, however, students should be aware that, if they change their mind, transferring to a standard program may require extra course work.

DECIDING ON A DEGREE

The level of graduate study needed to launch a successful psychology career varies with the area of specialization, but one general rule applies: The doctorate provides the job seeker with many more alternatives and opportunities for advancement than does the master's degree. In some areas, professional recognition depends on the degree held. The American Psychological Association (APA), for example, has several types of affiliations but reserves membership with full voting privileges for psychologists holding a doctorate. In addition, APA takes the position that the title "psychologist" used in certain applied areas of psychology should be limited to those who have completed their training from a doctoral program accredited by the APA. It is also the case that, in many states, licensing of psychologists is restricted to those holding a doctorate.

Most advanced degree programs in psychology are offered through psychology departments, although some programs can be found in education departments and departments with titles derived from the area of specialization, such as human services, counseling, and child and family development. Such programs confer the traditional Master of Arts (M.A.), Master of Science (M.S.), and Doctor of Philosophy (Ph.D.) degrees as well as the Master of Education (M.Ed.), Doctor of Education (Ed.D.), and Doctor of Psychology (Psy.D.).

The difficulty of gaining admission to graduate school varies according to the school and the specialization. Most graduate schools, especially those that emphasize research preparation, look for students with at least an overall B average in their major field and in related courses, and higher grades during their junior and senior years. In the most competitive programs—for example, doctoral programs in clinical psychology—students must be strong in all admission categories, with high grades (B+/A–), excellent test scores, strong letters of recommendation, and appropriate course work and experience, including research experience.

ACADEMIC PSYCHOLOGY

Academic psychologists represent all specializations within the field. Their common denominator is their employment in colleges and universities. These scholars enjoy studying and exploring their specialty in psychology, trying to learn more about it through research, and sharing what they know with their colleagues and their students.

In general, the academic job market is tight and highly competitive. Major universities have competitive graduate programs and want faculty who maintain active and ambitious research programs. Since research programs need financial support, psychologists at major universities must compete with other scholars for limited research funds. This requires them to write research proposals to government agencies, foundations, and other sources that support both basic and applied research. Teaching responsibilities at these institutions require faculty to divide their teaching between undergraduate and graduate students.

Faculty at colleges without research-oriented programs are not expected to do a significant amount of research, but rather to teach and stay informed of new developments in the field. Psychology faculty at such schools usually teach twice as many courses as their colleagues at research-oriented institutions. At community and junior colleges, the balance is tilted even further toward teaching and away from research.

Four-year colleges require faculty members to have a doctorate, but staff at junior and community colleges may include faculty with master's degrees or doctorates. Salaries for academic psychologists vary with the status of the person, the institution, the area of specialization, and the employing department. In general, academic salaries are lower than salaries of psychologists working in industry.

CLINICAL, COUNSELING, AND HUMAN SERVICES

Clinical Psychology

Clinical psychologists are responsible for the assessment and treatment of people who need help in dealing with psychological problems. Treatment populations may range from very young children to the elderly and may involve individual psychotherapy, work with families, groups, or couples. Assessment may be to determine a diagnosis or the appropriate form of treatment and may involve psychological testing to determine intelligence, identify learning and other cognitive disabilities, personality traits, achievement, and potential. Those in direct service roles have a private practice, work in hospitals or clinics, or function as part of a school, community, or service organization. Clinical psychologists also do consulting work with a variety of agencies and organizations. In industry, for example, they may set up programs to help families avoid adjustment problems when executives are transferred, to teach people how to deal with stress, or to provide alcohol and drug abuse assistance.

In addition to direct service and consulting, clinical psychologists frequently administer clinics, mental health agencies, rehabilitation facilities, hospital units, or counseling centers. Clinical psychologists are especially in demand when government funds designated for mental health activities are involved and when clinical interns, mental health workers, and clinicians with less than a doctorate need supervision. Licensing criteria in most states restrict the title "psychologist," for purposes of private practice or unsupervised work, to those who hold a doctorate in psychology. Though many mental health centers do rely heavily on professionals with a master's degree to provide direct client service, these master's level clinicians are supervised by the center's staff members who hold doctorates.

The doctorate level offers two different degree options in clinical psychology. The traditional Ph.D. combines clinical course and practicum training with additional emphasis on research skills related to clinical psychology. The Ph.D. program usually takes five to seven years to complete, including a required doctoral dissertation and a one-year internship. The Doctor of Psychology (Psy.D.) degree is relatively new and emphasizes clinical training, with a reduced emphasis on research. Students master research tools—statistics and research methodology, for example—but do not conduct extensive individual research projects such as a dissertation. Psy.D. programs can usually be completed in three to four years with a one-year internship.

Two types of master's degree options are available in clinical psychology. One is designed as preparation for the doctorate; the other provides a heavier emphasis on clinical training and assumes the student will terminate formal education with a master's degree and enter the field as a clinician.

A wide range of jobs and potential employers await clinical psychologists at both the master's and doctoral level. Students applying to clinical psychology doctoral programs should be aware, however, that the APA has developed standards for training clinical psychologists and accredits programs that meet these standards. Graduates from accredited programs have a clear advantage in the competition for internships and employment, and students should try to gain admission to an accredited program.

SAMPLE PROGRAM
Psychology Courses: introductory, statistics, research methods, abnormal, social, cognitive, biological, clinical, counseling, test and measurement, personality, psychopharmacology, research projects.

Related Courses: mathematics, computer science, sociology, biology, social work, anthropology, educational psychology.

Counseling Psychology

Counseling psychology differs from clinical psychology, though there is some overlap of professional skills. In fact, some hold that the overlap becomes greater each year. A major difference is the wide range of sub-specialties that are identified as counseling. Many of these do not involve nor require training in psychotherapy. Therefore, for our purposes, we will generalize that psychotherapy is the responsibility of the clinical psychologist while counseling psychologists are not trained to deal with the severe emotional problems of the client and do not try to achieve major personality changes with a client. Rather, the counseling psychologist works with people who have problems, helping them cope, identify options, and make reasonable choices. Counseling is concerned with adjustment and normal developmental problems as well as with the prevention of severe emotional problems.

The problem-solving orientation of counseling has led to such areas of specialization as marriage counseling, rehabilitation counseling, school counseling, and career counseling. Counselors work in a variety of settings, including mental health centers, halfway houses, religious centers, colleges, secondary and elementary schools, industry, rehabilitation facilities, and various social service agencies.

The job market varies with the counseling specialty, setting, location, and economic conditions. For example, increased costs and reluctance to increase taxes supporting school systems have resulted in a limited job market for elementary school counselors. Budget restrictions have also limited the opportunities for counselors at the college level, but to a lesser extent. Counseling positions do exist for people at all levels of training, but most professional positions require a graduate degree. For maximum career flexibility, the doctorate is recommended. Counseling is one of the specialties for which the APA provides a list of accredited doctoral programs and in which the title "psychologist" is restricted to those who hold a doctorate. Nevertheless, many counselors who hold only the master's degree can enjoy success in several specializations, including school counselor, rehabilitation counselor, career counselor, and counselors in college student personnel offices.

SAMPLE PROGRAM
Psychology Courses: introductory, statistics, research methods, abnormal, social, cognitive, biological, clinical, counseling, test and measurement, personality, psychopharmacology, research projects.

Related Courses: mathematics, computer science, sociology, biology, social work, anthropology, educational psychology.

Is the M.A. or Ph.D. Necessary?

Some opportunities in human service areas related to clinical or counseling psychology exist for those with a bachelor's or associate arts degree. A person with a bachelor's degree could teach psychology and social sciences in a secondary school. Some community colleges, colleges, and universities have established associate arts and bachelor's degree programs in mental health work. These programs help develop skills in counseling, behavior modification, interviewing, testing, and interpreting psychological tests. The jobs available to these trained individuals are under direct supervision of professionally trained psychologists or other mental health professionals.

Other jobs for which a human service orientation is highly regarded are found in settings such as schools, community centers, social service agencies, halfway houses, crisis intervention programs, youth services, and general outreach programs. Students with a bachelor's or associate arts degree in psychology have been hired as community relations officers, police officers, affirmative action officers, public safety officers, recreation workers, social workers, health educators, houseparents, rehabilitation counselors, youth and family counselors, psychiatric assistants, teacher aides, directors of volunteer services, community workers, probation and parole officers, sustaining case workers, residential youth specialists, foster home recruiters, case aide workers, camp directors, aging/rehabilitation specialists, vocational program coordinators, and program specialists for the developmentally disabled.

Career advancement for those without graduate degrees depends on the employing agency. Someone working in an agency staffed predominantly by professionals in mental health will probably find that the only way to advance in client service areas is to acquire the necessary professional credentials. Often, however, human service agencies are not administered by service professionals, and administrative advancement for bachelor's degree holders may be possible.

ALCOHOL AND DRUG ABUSE PROGRAMS

In the past, the most successful programs in alcohol and drug abuse were run by people who formerly were abusers. While many of these programs still exist and continue to be effective, psychologists have become increasingly involved, not only in direct treatment but also in training and in the planning and administration of treatment programs. Careers in treatment programs exist at all training levels and in a variety of settings. Hospitals, mental health agencies, and a growing number of corporations employ professionals in this field. Psychologists work with clients, clients' families, and in programs designed to promote organizational or public awareness.

A career in substance abuse research will require a graduate degree, and much of the research is conducted by academic psychologists. Opportunities in this area include testing effectiveness of treatment programs, studying social factors that contribute to abuse or rehabilitation, probing the connection between drugs and behavior, and exploring new types of treatment programs.

HEALTH PSYCHOLOGY

Health psychology, which is sometimes referred to as behavioral medicine, is concerned with understanding the relationship between physical problems and how people feel and behave. This has resulted in new career opportunities for psychologists interested in understanding, treating, and preventing medical problems. Psychologists with interest in this area may pursue their interests in different ways. For example, some interests may be related to social psychology with research on the effectiveness of public service messages in reducing teenage smoking or effective ways of changing attitudes about how mental illness is viewed. On the other hand, many psychologists have interest in direct service. They may teach relaxation techniques to insomniacs, develop weight control programs for obesity clinics, work with patients who suffer from severe headaches, develop programs to combat fear of dental treatment, or teach techniques on how to handle, reduce, or even eliminate certain kinds of pain.

Jobs in this new field are frequently available in hospital or clinical settings. Often, however, organizations hire psychologists to give workshops to their employees on topics such as stress management, and this preventive aspect of health psychology is handled equally by psychologists who are members of a hospital or clinic staff and those who are not affiliated with any medical facility.

Psychologists may also train and teach medical students, physicians, nurses, and other health professionals to understand relevant psychological information and use intervention techniques to provide more effective service to patients. This role for psychologists results in employment opportunities in medical schools, hospitals and clinics, and allied health programs such as health education, occupational therapy, and nursing.

Although most health psychology careers require doctoral training, some opportunities are available for those who have earned an associate arts, bachelor's, or master's degree. Weight control clinics and programs to help people stop smoking hire individuals from all levels if they have been trained in the appropriate techniques or have counseling skills. Hospitals also hire paraprofessionals who work with patients who are resisting treatment or to help patients adjust to the hospital setting. Drug and alcohol treatment programs use professionals at all degree levels and even some without degrees, as do some agencies specializing in treating geriatric patients.

COMMUNITY PSYCHOLOGY

Community psychologists recognize that social conditions and human relations can contribute to mental health problems. Their strategy assumes that steps can be taken within the community to attack or even prevent problem areas. For example, community psychologists might help members of a community develop a school program to involve parents, teachers, and students in dealing with drug problems from education and prevention to establishing a hotline for drug abusers. They may establish a counseling program for juvenile offenders designed to reduce the number of repeat offenders. They can be concerned with creating programs and experiences designed to help members of a community gain a sense of empowerment over their own future.

A community can be a neighborhood, a school, a town, a prison, or any such body of people. Thus, the community psychologist may be employed by any of a variety of institutions and organizations, such as government agencies, community mental health centers, universities, and correctional institutions. The community psychologist studies specific problems of the community and designs programs and strategies to deal with them. Direct service or intervention is usually left to the members of the community, to mental health service professionals, or to trained paraprofessionals. Because research involving program design and evaluation is a major responsibility of a community psychologist, a doctorate is the recommended level of training.

SAMPLE PROGRAM
Psychology Courses: introductory, statistics, research methods, social, personality, learning, cognitive, community psychology, gender issues in psychology, small-group behavior, adolescent psychology, abnormal psychology, community projects, research projects.

Related Courses: sociology, anthropology, social work, women's studies, political science, community health, mathematics, computer science.

FORENSIC PSYCHOLOGY

Psychology and law has become a popular area of interest in recent years. This specialization can be practiced by psychologists trained in any one of several areas of the field. However, most often, they have been trained in clinical, counseling, community, personality, or social psychology. In prisons, psychologists provide individual and group psychotherapy, help new inmates adjust to prison, provide profiles and evaluations used in making parole decisions, and suggest programs to make productive use of an inmate's time. Forensic psychologists also help train other prison staff, including teachers, guards, and correction officers, to work effectively with prisoners.

Psychologists who work with police departments may help establish selection criteria for police department applicants, and become involved in many aspects of the training program. They might, for example, teach strategies for effectively dealing with people in tense situations. In a more direct problem-solving role, forensic psychologists can provide insight into the personality and likely behavior of a criminal or help with plans for crowd control by applying group behavior research findings.

In less apparent direct service roles, forensic psychologists may hold responsibility for counseling adults and children in situations that are related to the legal system. For example, they may provide adjustment counseling for those involved in divorce proceedings or anger management for individuals who have been identified as abusive and whose spouse and/or children are in danger of being victimized.

Psychologists also work with the courts, to administer psychodiagnostic tests to determine whether a person is competent to stand trial, serve as expert witnesses in a variety of cases, provide information to lawyers, or advise judges on matters related to sentencing. They are frequently involved in cases concerning children or family disputes, including child custody cases.

In their research role, forensic psychologists study jury selection techniques, procedural fairness, witness accuracy and memory, and a number of related topics that have an impact on the judicial system. Applications of this research can be seen in high-profile court cases. Legal teams use forensic psychologists to help in profiling potential members of a jury. After a jury has been selected, forensic psychologists might assemble a group of people who psychologically resemble the actual jury to test the effectiveness of approaches to be used by the defense or prosecution.

Although most professionals who pursue careers in forensic psychology hold a doctorate, careers for others do exist. Jobs in corrections work, including corrections counseling positions, work in halfway houses, vocational counseling, and positions with programs serving juvenile offenders and drug offenders are open to people with a master's, bachelor's, or associate arts degree.

SAMPLE PROGRAM
Psychology Courses: introductory, statistics, research methods, abnormal, social, cognitive, biological, clinical, counseling, test and measurement, personality, psychopharmacology, research projects.

Related Courses: mathematics, computer science, sociology, biology, social work, anthropology, educational psychology.

DEVELOPMENTAL PSYCHOLOGY

Developmental psychologists study all aspects of psychological development over a life span from prenatal to old age. However, they are most interested in studying children because they develop and change so rapidly that it is easier to develop research approaches to study development. Most developmental psychology careers are in academic settings, where the main interest is in research and teaching. However, research opportunities also exist in other settings for those who hold an advanced degree. Foundations interested in child-related problems fund research in developmental psychology, as do toy companies trying to develop toys appropriate for various developmental stages. Psychologists are also hired by child- and parent-oriented magazines and television programs as consultants, writers, and researchers.

Federal agencies offer various kinds of employment for developmental psychologists with a graduate degree. A defense agency may be interested in day care, or an agricultural agency may need information on nutrition and development. Members of Congress use developmental psychologists as a source of information about child-related issues and for expert information on existing or proposed programs.

Job opportunities related to developmental psychology are available for those with a bachelor's degree but frequently require companion skills or knowledge. Openings may be direct service jobs in child-care or in a day care center. The opportunity for jobs in day care continues to expand as centers are established for infants, handicapped, and school-age children. Employment may also be found in parent education programs run through local social service agencies, churches, child advocacy organizations, and hospital child-life programs.

More recently, developmental psychologists are found with interest in or working with the aging population. For example, developmental psychologists might be interested in memory, the effect of exercise on cognitive skills, or ways to slow degenerative processes. Those interested in direct service look to develop ways for elderly people to stay healthy and remain independent as long as possible.

SAMPLE PROGRAM
Psychology Courses: introductory, statistics, research methods, developmental, cognitive, biological, psycholinguistics, personality, social, gerontology, infancy, and learning.

Related Courses: mathematics, computer science, family studies, biological sciences, linguistics, sociology, education, speech, and hearing.

EDUCATIONAL PSYCHOLOGY/ SCHOOL PSYCHOLOGY

Educational psychologists' careers are tightly tied to the university setting. Educational psychology uses knowledge from all areas of psychology to study topics related to learning, the methods of instruction, the learning environment, teacher morale, and other factors that affect the education setting.

Because counseling programs are frequently a part of the educational psychology department in a university, counselor training can also be included here as a career option. However, counseling psychology programs should not be confused with another applied training program, school psychology, which also usually is a part of educational psychology departments. Careers of educational psychologists essentially mirror those of psychologists in psychology departments studying in related areas.

School psychologists, trained to identify problems in a school or class or with a particular student, give and interpret aptitude, achievement, and personality tests. Although they may have counseling skills, school psychologists are frequently relieved of that role. Instead, they test students who are suspected of having learning or behavior problems, interpret the tests, and meet with teachers, parents, and school staff to discuss the child's problems and recommend action to address the problems.

The school psychologist may also serve as a consultant to a teacher who is having problems with a class. After observing the situation, the psychologist may make recommendations for dealing with individuals or the class as a whole. School psychologists consult with professionals involved in programs for the handicapped, mentally retarded, mentally disturbed, and other special needs groups and both plan and evaluate the effectiveness of these programs.

A graduate degree is required for this profession. Master's degree and specialist's programs provide appropriate training, but the American Psychological Association has recommended the doctorate for those who use the title "school psychologist." States differ in their requirements for certifying school psychologists, and some require that the psychologist also be a certified teacher.

SAMPLE PROGRAM (School Psychologists)
Psychology Courses: introductory, statistics, research methods, social, abnormal, personality, learning, biological, cognitive, tests and measurement, individual intelligence testing, developmental, clinical or counseling.

Related Courses: special education, teacher education (reading), sociology, biology, mathematics, computer science, anthropology.

SPORT PSYCHOLOGY

Sport psychology is a new and expanding field, and sport psychologists specialize in psychological factors that affect an athlete's performance, such as why skilled athletes lose their ability to perform adequately in pressure situations, how anxiety affects performance, or what effect spectators have on a performance. Sport psychologists with research interests are usually in physical education or kinesiology departments at universities where they teach and learn. Some faculty also serve as consultants to sports teams.

Students building credentials as a sport psychologist usually will earn a graduate degree from a physical education program in sport psychology or earn a degree in counseling psychology with a specialization in sport psychology. Academic positions are not plentiful and, though a new field like this might lead to improving job opportunities, students should not expect a wide-open job market. Those who prepare for the field with a counseling degree provide themselves with additional job opportunities. A doctorate is necessary for a faculty position in a research university and is desirable for other positions.

In addition to doing research, sport psychologists run workshops and clinics for coaches on how to apply psychological principles to coaching. They also teach psychological training methods to groups of athletes through local hospitals, schools, and recreation centers. Some sport psychologists serve on the coaching staffs of major college athletic programs, professional teams, or Olympic teams. They work with the team's staff to plan effective coaching strategies and devise methods for keeping the team in an appropriate frame of mind. They also work with the team as a group, teaching techniques for keeping emotions under control and maintaining concentration. Finally, they work with individual team members to apply the general psychology skills to specific problems or likely game situations.

INDUSTRIAL/ORGANIZATIONAL PSYCHOLOGY

Although industrial psychologists are concerned with all aspects of the organization, their primary responsibilities are the recruitment, selection, training, and evaluations of employees, and for these tasks they require psychological measurement and test development knowledge. The industrial psychologist seeks to ensure that the job applicants are screened properly, employee selections are based on valid and reliable test data, new people are trained in the shortest possible time, and effective methods are established for judging workers' performance and selecting those who deserve to be promoted.

Industrial psychologists also develop programs to foster a positive attitude among employees. They study motivation, arrange procedures for resolving conflicts within the organization, and establish leadership training sessions.

Organizational psychologists differ from industrial psychologists in that they are more concerned with groups instead of individuals. For example, how can one division within the organization work more effectively with another? If there is conflict between groups, or if a particular manager is having difficulty with people under his/her charge, the organizational psychologist could develop a strategy to reduce the conflict between groups or help the manager to develop a more effective style or approach in dealing with employees.

Industrial/organizational psychologists work for large corporations, in private practice as consultants, and on the faculty of business schools, psychology departments, or labor relations institutes. In recent years, the trend has been for major corporations to rely more on hiring consultants rather than keep a staff of industrial psychologists. However, this does not mean that the employment picture has diminished. In fact, there is a strong demand for industrial/organizational psychologists and the financial benefits are usually quite good. Most major corporations and consulting firms want industrial psychologists with a doctorate. In fact, the American Psychological Association has required the doctorate if the title "psychologist" is used in this area. At the master's degree level, the role of the psychologist is usually limited to a small number of specific topic areas, such as testing, selection, and job evaluation. At the bachelor's level, available jobs include test administration, data collection, interviewing, and perhaps some work in support of the test development staff. Salaries are generally very good for industrial psychologists, with the highest salaries being held by psychologists associated with consulting firms.

SAMPLE PROGRAM
Psychology Courses: introductory, statistics, research methods, social industrial, learning, human factors, personality, tests and measurement, motivation, personnel.

Related Courses: mathematics, computer science, economics, sociology, accounting, industrial relations, business administration.

SOCIAL PSYCHOLOGY/CONSUMER PSYCHOLOGY/ENVIRONMENTAL PSYCHOLOGY

Social psychology is the study of individual and group social behavior. The career most often associated with this specialization is a research career in an academic setting, but research positions also exist in foundations and philanthropic organizations, government agencies, political organizations, and community social service agencies. It is also obvious from the discussion of other areas of specialization that the interests of social psychologists can be applied to careers such as industrial psychology, sport psychology, educational psychology, etc.

Marketing research positions, especially with large corporations and advertising agencies, are open to well-trained social psychologists. Consumer psychologists are interested in many of the same questions that social psychologists study but apply the questions to consumer-related topics. They study buying behavior, resistance to persuasion, children's ability to persuade parents, how to influence purchasing, how one's life or work influences buying, etc. Although many consumer psychologists work for industry, positions also exist with consumer advocate groups and government agencies. A doctorate is usually required for employment as a consumer psychologist.

Environmental psychologists are concerned with the way our physical environment affects people and how people may affect our environment. Environmental psychologists study housing issues, the effects of crowding on different types of populations, personal space issues, and how these issues affect and are affected by attitudes. They also study the effects of temperature, noise, pollution, lighting, color, work space on the quality of life, effectiveness of work activities, and moods and temperament.

Other fields that use social psychology knowledge include teaching, recreation, social work, communication fields, and environmental related fields. In fact, many undergraduate and graduate academic programs outside of psychology require their students to take social psychology courses and have social psychologists as members of their own faculty.

SAMPLE PROGRAM
Psychology Courses: introductory, statistics, research methods, social personality, cognitive, perception and sensory processes, social cognition, attitude theory, tests and measurement, thinking, learning, memory, research projects.

Related Courses: mathematics, computer science, sociology, anthropology, biological sciences, advertising, marketing.

QUANTITATIVE/MEASUREMENT PSYCHOLOGY

Quantitative psychology is concerned with the methodology for behavior research. Psychologists in this field develop methods of data analysis for the study of individual differences in ability, personality, and other psychological phenomena. Quantitative psychologists may also be interested in developing models of various psychological processes and structures, such as impression formation, judgment formation, memory, and so on.

One branch of quantitative psychology is measurement psychology. Experts called psychometricians measure psychological traits, states, and constructs such as motivation, intelligence, and attitudes. Their knowledge, instruments, approaches, and applications play an important role in all applied areas of psychology.

Many jobs in quantitative psychology and psychometrics require a doctorate, including those in consulting firms, academic settings, government agencies, and market research organizations. Graduates with a master's degree will find a healthy job market with test development companies and with the personnel/human resources divisions of organizations, as well as in marketing research, advertising, and government work, including civil service agencies. At the bachelor's degree level, paraprofessional jobs do exist with government civil service agencies and corporations that need people to help design tests and analyze and interpret test data. These jobs are under the supervision of those with graduate training in measurement and require the appropriate psychology background as well as a good background in mathematics and computer science.

SAMPLE PROGRAM
Psychology Courses: introductory, statistics, research methods, social personality, perception/sensation, cognitive, mathematical models in psychology, tests and measurement, industrial psychology, motivation.

Related Courses: mathematics, computer science, education.

HUMAN-FACTORS/ENGINEERING PSYCHOLOGY

Human-factors psychologists, sometimes called engineering psychologists, specialize in the way people interact with environments, systems, and products. They use the scientific study of human behavior and experience to understand, design, or improve person-machine systems so that systems function safely and productively. They contribute, for example, to the design of military equipment, space vehicles, airplanes, computer terminals and programs, communication equipment, consumer products, and transportation systems. Some human-factors psychologists are concerned with training methods, safety and accident prevention systems, and work environments (including light, space, and color). In the health field they may work on emergency room design, prosthetic devices, or health care delivery systems.

Human-factors psychologists work for government agencies, private industry, not-for-profit institutions, and consulting firms; in addition, they teach and do research in university settings. Salaries for human-factors psychologists are excellent, with jobs in industry and consulting firms paying the highest salaries and college and university positions the lowest.

Opportunities are available for people with a master's degree or doctoral degree. Some bachelor's degree level jobs are available each year but they are scattered. Although they pay well, careers in human-factors psychology would be difficult to obtain without a graduate degree.

SAMPLE PROGRAM
Psychology Courses: introductory, statistics, research methods, learning, cognitive, perception, social industrial, human factors, tests and measurement, information processing, engineering psychology, artificial intelligence.

Related Courses: mathematics, computer science, industrial engineering, physics, physiology.

BIOLOGICAL PSYCHOLOGY AND NEUROPSYCHOLOGY

Biological psychology studies the biological basis of human behavior. Though careers in this field are almost all in research settings, they are not confined to universities. Both government agencies and private research institutes, many of which are located in or near Washington, D.C., provide career opportunities for biological psychologists. Pharmaceutical companies also hire psychologists for research in psychopharmacology.

Neuropsychologists are interested in many of the same topics of interest to biological psychologists. We separate them here because many neuropsychologists also diagnose and treat problems related to the central nervous system. This includes teaching patients to acquire and process information in new ways.

The overall job market is weighted heavily in favor of those who hold a doctorate, with a few research positions available for those with a master's degree. Even with the doctorate, a person interested in a research career in biological psychology will find a very tight job market. However, biological psychology provides an excellent background for medical students and for those interested in science writing and science journalism. Clinical neuropsychologists work in research settings but also in hospitals and clinics in neurology and psychiatry units.

SAMPLE PROGRAM
Psychology Courses: introductory, statistics, biological research methods, biological, perception, cognitive, developmental, abnormal, memory/amnesia, psychopharmacology, clinical psychology, neuropsychology.

Related Courses: mathematics, computer science, chemistry, biological sciences, neuroscience.

EVALUATION RESEARCH

A career possibility that cuts across several areas of psychology is evaluation research. Organizations, agencies, and communities are continuing established programs on the assumption that they are achieving their desired ends; in fact, few of these organizations know if the programs are really working. In recent years many have hired program evaluators to determine whether such programs do, in fact, work. Psychologists, because of their training in experimental design and quantitative research, are among the scientists sought after to do evaluation research. The skills required for a career in evaluation research are almost always developed in doctoral programs; career opportunities for people with lesser degrees are virtually nonexistent.